CRIME
IN
HERTFORDSHIRE

Volume One

Law and Disorder
from Anglo-Saxon England
to the Present

Simon Walker

First published March 2002
by
The Book Castle
12 Church Street
Dunstable
Bedfordshire
LU5 4RU

The right of Simon Walker to be identified as the Author of this work has been asserted by him in accordance with the Copyright, Designs and Patents Act, 1988.

ISBN 1 903747 13 9

In Preparation:
Crime in Hertfordshire: Volume Two: Murder and Misdeeds

Printed by Antony Rowe Ltd., Bumper's Farm, Chippenham, Wiltshire, SN14 6LH

Contents

Acknowledgements

A number of people and organisations have greatly assisted in the preparation of this book. Particular thanks are due to the following: the staff at Hertfordshire Archives and Local Studies, always helpful and prepared to answer the most inane questions; Bedford County Library, who made available books I could not find in Hertfordshire; Rosemary Bennett at Hertford Museum, whose knowledge of the town and its history is so extensive; Anne Wheeler at the Museum of St. Albans, who was almost embarrassingly generous with her time and willingness to help. Gill Riding and Jo Benson at Hitchin Museum were as helpful as they always are; Sally Ackroyd of Stevenage Museum; and Inspector Steve Kourik of Hertfordshire Constabulary, who made available documents and artefacts belonging to the force's Historical Society. Finally I must thank Scilla Douglas, who kept an eye open on my behalf in the course of her own energetic research. To those mentioned, and to all the others who have given their time so freely, I should like to say thank you.

About the Author

Simon Walker has lived in Hertfordshire all his life. He was born in Hitchin in 1950, and was educated at Hitchin Boys' Grammar School. After a career in computing in the financial sector, he retired in 1999 in order to concentrate on local history. He has written two other books: *The Bridewells of Hitchin,* and *Underground Hitchin.* He is currently working on a companion volume to *Crime in Hertfordshire: Law and Disorder*, consisting of a collection of criminal cases from the county, entitled *Crime in Hertfordshire: Murder and Misdeeds.*

Introduction

It is hard to imagine a society without some code of conduct, and the means to enforce it. From early tribal customs to the complex legal system of the 20th century is an enormous leap; or rather, many small steps. Sometimes one pace forward and two back, but with an overall trend to complexity and confusion. By 1950 it was a courageous person who could claim to know exactly what was or was not legal, and many people broke one law or another without even being aware of it. They still do.

English law has a long, almost unbroken history, and it is better documented than most. There are the legal codes of the Anglo-Saxons, and from the works of Ranulf de Glanvill of the 12th century onward there are legal textbooks. Many documents have been preserved, including Quarter Sessions and Assize rolls, prison calendars, registers, receipts, manor records, vestry minutes and so on. Pamphlets and newspapers of the past report crimes in considerable and often gruesome detail.

The origins of some institutions and practices are unfortunately unrecorded, and we can only speculate. But all is not lost. By making comparisons with the legal systems of other countries and societies, some of the missing material can be implied. On some issues there is disagreement amongst authorities, and where this is the case I have opted for what seems to me to be the most likely of the alternatives. The responsibility for any errors is therefore mine.

Throughout history men have dominated the whole field of crime and punishment. Men made the laws, and it was predominantly men who broke them. If therefore I use the word "he" when I should say "he or she," I apologise.

It is not my intention to write a textbook, but a readable, and, I hope, interesting account of a fascinating subject. In order to achieve this I have had to omit some of the detail I have gathered, often with some regret. I have I hope included enough examples of offences to satisfy all but the greediest of readers. Those who wish to do so may like to use the bibliography as a starting point for further reading.

Law and order consists of a number of elements: the forces of law and order, the courts, and the prisons; the sentences handed down, and the methods of punishment employed. The last is sometimes gruesome, but I am afraid that is the nature of the subject. Wherever possible I have used examples from our own county, but if on occasion I have had to stray across borders I hope I may be forgiven. I have chosen not to go beyond the end of the Second World War in most cases, because the legislation since that time has been so frequent that it merits a book on its own.

The laws of the countries forming the United Kingdom vary, and it is for this reason alone that I have used the term 'English law' throughout this book. Hertfordshire is probably as English as you can get.

I considered modernising spellings when quoting from various sources, but chose not to; if a word is not obvious, try reading it aloud - its meaning soon becomes clear. All quotations are in English, though many legal documents were written in medieval French or Latin (with a brief interlude during the Commonwealth in the 17th century).

There are sometimes occasions when I have used terms without explaining them fully. In these cases, a full explanation appears in the chapter that deals with that subject (for example trial by ordeal is mentioned in the *Law of the Land*, and covered in detail in *Courts and Trials*).

Near the end of the book I have included a glossary of the terms that caused me so much bewilderment during my research.

I have used the weights and measures in use at the time. A conversion chart appears next to the glossary.

Finally, if there is one thing that I have learned from working on this book it is the sheer waste over the centuries. Not only the victims of the crimes, but the criminals too; and those left to pick up the pieces behind both.

Chapter One

The Law Of The Land

The criminal law is nowadays taken to mean the law relating to the definition, trial and punishment of crimes. A crime is an act forbidden by law that harms the state or its subjects. The criminal law in Hertfordshire is of course the criminal law of England. There are bylaws unique to certain areas, but these usually relate to non-criminal matters (though penalties may result from disobeying them).

It is important to bear in mind that the law, the courts and the machinery for its enforcement were not planned as a single entity; rather, they grew on an ad hoc basis over the course of centuries. This helps to explain some of the anomalies that came to pass.

The Anglo-Saxon Period: the 7th century to 1066

The Anglo-Saxons brought with them the laws of lower Germany of the dark ages, and it is upon these laws that the later codes of their Kings were based. Most other European countries have systems based on ecclesiastical (Canon) and Roman law. England is different. What Roman law was left in England at the start of the dark ages was swept away by succeeding invaders, and because of the both secular and ecclesiastical isolation of these islands, the influence of neither Roman nor Canon law had as great an impact as elsewhere in Europe. Other influences though are detectable to a minor extent. Elements of Danish law appeared for example, especially in northern and eastern England. There seems to be very little trace of Celtic codes however, other than a similarity in the customs of blood feuds and atonement for wrongs.

There is a surprisingly large quantity of Anglo-Saxon criminal law still existing; in total, 419 paragraphs from the codes of a number of Kings. Of these paragraphs, 238 are concerned with tariffs of fines, 80 refer to capital and corporal punishment, outlawry (withdrawal of the protection of the law), and confiscation of goods, and 101 are rules of procedure in the administration of the law.

The codes, or parts of them, of the following Kings have been preserved: Aethelbert, Hlothhere, Eadric, Wihtred, Ine, Alfred the Great, Edward the Elder, Aethelstan, Edmund, Edgar, Aethelred and Cnute, ranging from the 7th to 11th centuries. Some codes relied upon earlier ones, so we know that Offa too compiled a code; Alfred says that he drew upon it when formulating his own. There are similarities too between Alfred and older Frankish laws. He selected those he liked, and those he did not he rejected. With disarming modesty he says "I dared not presume to set in writing at all many [laws] of my own, because it was unknown to me what would please those who should come after us."

Despite this display of humility, some of the punishments were draconian. Ine of West Sussex set the penalty for not having a child baptised within thirty days at thirty shillings. If the child then died unbaptised, the father forfeited everything he possessed. Wihtred decreed that "if any stranger shall wander privately through the country, and shall neither cry aloud nor sound his horn, he shall be taken for a thief, and shall be either slain or banished." Athaelstan's code said that "in the case of a female slave, who commits an act of theft anywhere, except against her master or mistress, sixty and twenty female slaves shall go and bring three logs each and burn that one slave." In contrast, other Anglo-Saxon penalties seem lenient. A murder could be atoned for by the payment of a fine, called 'wer-gild,' to the victim's kin.

The King made the law in association with his advisors, the 'Witenagemot,' whose members, both lay and clerical, were appointed by him. The Witenagemot was also the highest judicial body in the country, and tried cases as well as advising the King in the making of law.

In addition to these legal codes there were rules and rights laid down by custom, called folk-rights. The King had the power to amend folk-rights as he saw fit.

By the middle of the 11th century, these procedures had evolved into an early feudal system. A new penal system arose, based on a system of punishments, ranging from death to financial penalties. Fines were carefully graded, based upon the offence and the status of the offender.

Though Aethelbert's code of around 600 AD was predominantly a list of such fines, it also defines procedures for claiming the right of sanctuary. This means of escaping justice, which was to last for a thousand years, was less easily invoked than is generally believed. The fugitive had to fulfil a number of requirements: he had to

- confess his crime to the clergy.
- surrender any weapons he had with him.
- obey the rules of the religious order from whom he is claiming sanctuary.
- pay a fee.
- give under oath full details of his crime.
- go before the coroner, clothed in sackcloth, within forty days, confess, and take an oath to leave the realm.

He had then to move quickly, for little time was allowed to reach a port. Sanctuary for criminal acts was abolished by James I in 1623.

In early Anglo-Saxon times, the keeping of the King's Peace was based on kinship. A wrong was avenged by the victim's family, or compensation was paid to them by the offender. A fine might also be payable to the Crown. Either the victim or his family was responsible for bringing the prosecution - there was no central body for the prosecution of crimes. After all, why should the state take an interest in crimes against the individual? It was not until the last quarter of the 19th century that the nation assumed responsibility for criminal prosecution; and the option of private prosecution is still available.

Kinship could also work the other way. Kindred were jointly responsible for the actions of any one of them. This system gradually gave way to voluntary associations, or guilds, but still functioning in the same manner. By the 10th century an obligatory system called frankpledge was in place, consisting of men in groups called 'tithes,' jointly responsible for the behaviour of the others.

The Norman Conquest

The position of William I in 1066 was the same as that of many an invader, before or since. He had a large population to govern, and a relatively small occupation army. His intention, initially at least, seems to have been to adopt the easiest option when it came to legal matters - with minor changes only, he would let English laws govern the English people. The Crown was obviously to be the supreme judicial authority via the King's Court, but beneath it he used the existing administrative system - the Shire and Hundred Courts. Indeed, it was this legal system that was used to gather the information that led to the Domesday Book. All authority of these courts was derived from the King.

It was not for a hundred years that any serious modification of Anglo-Saxon law started, and it took a further hundred years to complete it. Thus central government became Norman, whilst local government remained Anglo-Saxon, albeit in a submissive form. Perhaps the major change in the administration of justice the average Anglo-Saxon would have seen was the fall from grace of the ealdorman, and the corresponding rise of the sheriff, who became the King's principal representative in the shire. One of his principal duties was the collection of fines from offenders.

If the system was the same, its equity in application was not. The Anglo-Saxon was now a second-class citizen, and he had better not forget it. If for example a man should be found killed, the hundred had either to prove that the body was not that of a Norman, produce the killer, or pay a punitive fine.

Offences were divided into two classes - misdemeanours and felonies. A misdemeanour was a minor offence, meriting corporal punishment or a fine. A felony was a crime that (originally at least) attracted the death penalty. This division remained until 1967.

Above: the hundreds of Hertfordshire. 1. Tring; 2. Dacorum; 3. Cashio; 4. Hitchin; 5. Broadwater; 6. Odsey; 7. Edwinstree; 8. Braughin; 9.Hertford. Note that Dacorum is divided by Cashio. (author)

Henry I attempted in the early 12th century to codify the law as it had existed under Edward the Confessor, in order to restore confidence following the tyranny of William Rufus. The result was the *Legis Henrici Primi.* He was only partially successful, and the book in fact drew more upon the code of Cnute. In part Henry's aim was to strengthen the unity of his kingdom by encouraging the cult of Edward, upon whom the Norman claim to the English throne relied. Edward was seen, perhaps romantically, as the ideal of kingship, and Henry's desire to become identified with him was a shrewd move. Edward was canonised in 1161, and his body enshrined in Westminster Abbey.

Henry I will also be remembered for the list of penalties for swearing within the precincts of the royal residence:

dukes	40 shillings
lords	20 shillings
squires	10 shillings

yeomen	3s 4d (half a mark)
pages	a whipping

The period of the Anarchy that followed Henry's death in 1135 saw bands of brigands roaming the countryside. The Anarchy it was called and anarchy it was; law and order broke down completely in some parts of the country. Local lords sided either with King Stephen or the Empress Matilda, and small castles were thrown up far and wide (examples exist at Great Wymondley and Pirton).

Magna Carta and Beyond

Under Henry II the courts were much reformed as will be explained later. Perhaps the next significant event was in 1215.

The importance of the Magna Carta has long been a subject for dispute. From the constitutional point of view, its chief impact was the curtailment of the king's power over his barons. They were granted irrevocable rights and privileges; despite later attempts to reject Magna Carta, the power of the crown was never to be the same again. The charter was forced on King John, and after signing it he tried to repudiate it. It was reissued following his death in 1216, with some amendments. From the legal standpoint it has some interesting and relevant clauses:

Clauses 20-22:	"Amercements (fines) are to be in accordance with the measure of the offence. They are not to be so heavy, in the case of grievous crimes, as to deprive any man of his means of livelihood. They are to be assessed by the honest men of the neighbourhood." Fines upon the clergy were only to be based on lands they held as laymen.
Clause 39:	"No freeman shall be taken, or imprisoned... or in any way destroyed... except by legal judgement of his peers or by the law of the land."
Clause 40:	"To no one will we sell, deny or delay right of justice."
Clause 42:	"All persons are free to come and go in time of peace, except outlaws and prisoners."
Clause 45:	"No justice, constable, sheriff or bailiff is to be appointed but that he knows the law and is willing to observe it." Rather alarmingly, this clause was omitted in the 1216 re-issue.
Clause 54:	"No one is to be taken or imprisoned upon the appeal of a woman for the death of any other than her husband." One wonders about the events leading to the inclusion of this clause.

Law and Disorder in Hertfordshire

Also mentioned in Magna Carta is the forerunner of the writ of *habeas corpus*, namely the writ *de odio et atiâ,* which "must not be refused." Both these writs are concerned with illegal imprisonment, and played an important part in allowing the accused to avoid trial by battle, and obtain a trial by jury. They also helped curb abuses of power by state servants.

An early form of consumer protection in the form of standard measures for ale is covered by Magna Carta. It was complemented fifty years later by a piece of legislation called the Assize of Bread and Ale. The price of these commodities was regulated against the price of corn and malt, and offenders punished with a fine. Transgressors appeared before the Manor or Borough Courts; Julia le Melleward was prosecuted four times in Wymondley in 1275, and fined one penny on each occasion.

Henry of Bracton, one of Henry III's justices in the first half of the 13th century, extracted from court records precedents to be followed. The result was a book of some 500 previous decisions. Then as now, there was no code as such; the law was a combination of precedent, statute law and the common law, which originated from custom and existing practice. Copies were made of Bracton's manuscript, and were used throughout the Kingdom. The effect was to stem the uncontrolled growth in complexity of the judicial system.

Under Henry's successor, Edward I, the legal system took on the form it was to retain for centuries to come. The next few years saw the enactment of some extremely important statutes, amongst them the two Statutes of Westminster, in 1275 and 1285, the Statute of Gloucester in 1278, and the Statute of Winchester, in 1285.

The Statute of Winchester, which was concerned with maintenance of the King's Peace, is covered later in the chapter on law enforcement.

The first Statute of Westminster 1275 consisted of many clauses, covering such matters as excessive fines, common right being due to all, poor as well as rich, abuse of wardship and so on. The other statutes were concerned with the administration of justice and enforcement, and are covered in later chapters.

Until the Treason Act of 1351, there was no firm definition of this offence, though it had been mentioned in several of the pre-Norman codes. It was left to the King and his justices to decide what the offence actually was. The new act divided treason into high treason and petty treason.

High treason consisted of several offences, all involving plotting against, or violation or murder of, the King, his family or his judicial officers; and counterfeiting of coinage, or importing counterfeit coins.

Petty treason was defined as the slaying of a master by his servant, a man by his wife, or a prelate by a man owing him allegiance.

Other offences were added to the list of treasons over the years to come. The penalty was to be drawn, hanged and quartered for men; women were to be burned. Henry VIII made poisoning an act of treason in 1531 and amended the punishment to "deth by boylynge." The burning of women was abolished in 1790.

By the end of the 15th century the Common Law was reasonably well defined, with a number of treatises on the subject being published. The numbers were set to expand, as during the last quarter of the century William Caxton had set up his printing press in Westminster. The principles of precedent and equity were established.

The 16th & 17th Centuries

The 14th and 15th centuries, whilst changes to the court structure occurred, had seen little in the way of new law. Such changes as there were tended to be of a minor nature. In the 16th and 17th centuries the pace began to hot up. It was an eventful period in the history of the nation, and there was legal and constitutional progress. More documents have survived from this period too, so we have more detail of individual cases.

Henry VIII's reign saw the beginning of the hysteria against witchcraft in England. The witch-hunts had begun earlier in the rest of Europe; executions were common by the late 15th century, when Pope Innocent VIII issued his Bull against witches. Two years later, Jacob Sprenger and Heinrich Kramer produced the *Malleus Maleficarum* – the *Hammer of Witches* – that stoked up the flames for more than two hundred years. Witchcraft was heresy, and heresy often meant death by burning.

In England heresy was usually treated as a relatively minor offence before the 14th century, but with the rise of John Wyclif's followers, who were known as Lollards, it was taken more seriously. Some were burned, but Wyclif himself had died in 1384. As a symbolic gesture his remains were exhumed in 1411, reduced to ashes, and thrown into a stream. Fortunately prosecutions for heresy never reached the scale they did in continental Europe under the inquisition.

But in England, before 1542, as in the rest of Europe, heresy was the only offence under which witches might be prosecuted. The Witchcraft Act of that year made some aspects of the craft a felony, punishable by death by hanging, without benefit of clergy. Attempted witchcraft, or minor offences, attracted the pillory and imprisonment for the first offence, and death thereafter. When Henry died in 1547 the act was repealed, only to be restored by Elizabeth I in 1559. An even more draconian act was passed by James I, forbidding all forms of conjuration, sorcery, enchantment and invocation of spirits on pain of death.

Law and Disorder in Hertfordshire

Here are some examples of witchcraft prosecutions from Hertfordshire:

1590   Elena, or Ellen, Brown and Mary Burges - found not guilty of murder, but guilty of the bewitching of animals, and sentenced to a year in prison and four appearances in the pillory.

1591   Joan White, of Bushey, wife of Thomas White, of Bushey, labourer, "a common witch and enchantress", for "devilishly bewitching Marion Man, daughter of William Man, of Bushey, tailor, through which she languished exceedingly from 20th December until 27th June next following when she died at Bushey." The Grand Jury's verdict was that Joan White feloniously killed Marion. She was acquitted at the Summer Session of Hertford Assizes. In 1595 a woman of the same name, perhaps the same person, was found guilty of witchcraft and the enchantment of goods. She received a year in prison and four appearances in the pillory.

1598   Mary Taylor of Hertford, for bewitching to death Simon Grubb. Joan and Frauncis Grub laid the charge. Mary was found guilty. The Assize Roll records that she had no goods and was hanged.

In these examples it is interesting that, even though the offence of witchcraft itself attracted serious penalties, the emphasis is on the harm done, rather than the harnessing of supernatural powers. This is typical of English trials, and quite unlike those of Continental Europe.

The chance of acquittal depended to a large degree upon the sitting justice. Some were confessed sceptics, such as Sir John Holt, whilst others allowed their own beliefs to cloud their judgement. The judge's summing up could make all the difference. Michael Dalton, in his book 'The Country Justice' of 1618, made a most alarming recommendation to his peers. Justices, he said, must not always expect direct evidence against witches "...seeing that their works are the works of darknesse, and no witnesses present with them to accuse them." Because the offence was committed secretly, he said, the level of proof required should be lower. The result was that the testimony of a single witness, or of young children was often accepted, and people lost their lives as a result.

Other clandestine crimes were of course equally difficult to prove, but fortunately common sense prevailed in most of those cases.

How many people were executed throughout England in these two hundred years is uncertain. Estimates range from less than 1,000 to over 30,000. Assize records, though incomplete, support the lower figure.

Henry VIII was succeeded by Edward VI, who was only ten years old when he came to the throne; he had little time to make an impact on the nation. When he died his half-sister Mary I became queen. She was a Catholic, and attempted to reverse the Protestant conversion of the country. For the period of 1553-58 to be a Protestant was to be a heretic, and the punishment for that was death by burning. About 300 people were executed, including some Hertfordshire men.

Vagrancy had always been connected in the minds of those in authority with criminality. In early days merely being a vagrant brought suspicion of being a fugitive serf. Later, the wanderer was suspected of being a criminal rather than a runaway. Contemporary opinion was that vagabonds formed a loose-knit criminal fraternity, combining to commit a crime or crimes, then splitting up and moving on. In 1495 local authorities were ordered to seek out "vagaboundes, idell and suspecte persones lyvyng suspeciously" and put them in the stocks for three days on a diet of bread and water, followed by expulsion from the township.

In 1530, whipping was permitted as an alternative punishment. Any vagrant within the terms of the Act was to be hauled to the nearest market place "and there tied to the end of a cart naked, and beaten with whips... till the body shall be bloody with such whipping." This was the punishment called "whipping at the cart's tail."

Soon afterwards mutilation was sanctioned, either by branding or cropping part of the offender's right ear. If convicted for a third time, he or she could be executed.

The end of the century saw all fortune-tellers, tinkers, peddlers, jugglers and the like classed as vagabonds, unless they "belonged to any Baron of this realm or any other honourable person of greater degree." A few years later the option of transportation of vagabonds beyond the seas was given to the courts.

1662 saw the passing of the Act of Settlement. It provided for the returning of paupers and vagrants to their parish of settlement - their 'home' parish - if they were likely to become a financial burden to the overseers of the poor.

More closely related to the Poor Laws than criminal law, this act is of interest insofar as it resulted in vagrants being flogged from parish to parish.

In 1697 an act was passed ruling that every pauper and his family on relief must wear a large cloth 'P' on their sleeve proclaiming their status. Lest this be thought a new idea, in 1345 Edward I had ordered a similar means of identification for prostitutes.

Hertfordshire, lying as it does across several major roads, and close to London, was not without its share of vagrants, vagabonds and rogues, and the following examples merely scratch the surface:

1588	Richard Fotte, of Westmill, labourer	He is "an idell and vagrante fellowe," who does not work to keep himself, but "lyvyth vere suspicyouslye."
1589	Thomas and Alice Gill	Sentenced at St. Albans for being "rogues."
1656	Joane Phillip	Late of Preston-on-the-Hill, Northamptonshire. She was "whipped according to law" at Broxbourne and passed on by Thomas Turner, constable of Pirton. (Whipping of female vagrants was discontinued in 1792).
1785	Elizabeth Maccarty	Sentenced to be publicly whipped as an incorrigible rogue.

Above: "whipped until the back be bloody..." note the use of the cat o' nine tails, and the man hanging from the scaffold in the background. (from a contemporary print)

The passing of vagrants became a living for some; the Robinson family had a contract with St. Albans from about 1720, and charged £200 per annum. As late as 1839, the constables of Barnet reported they had "whippt and passed three women and eight men last month onto Bedford and yᵉ Stroud."

For some of the vagrants, being passed from parish to parish had fatal results. Walter Cherry, of Hoddesdon, churchwarden, and Richard Simonds, constable of Broxbourne, appeared in court for "by the colour of their offices, removing an unknown woman, who was heavy with child, from Broxbourne to Ware, thereby causing her death." Vagrants from Hertfordshire were at risk in other parts of the country. In 1691, William Warden, of Cheshunt, a currier, was whipped by the parson and churchwardens of Whitchurch on Dartmoor, and ordered to be returned to Cheshunt. He died on horseback as he was being conveyed over Black Down.

Alehouse and innkeepers were required to report to the local constable the names, descriptions and dwelling places of any travellers staying at their establishments within two days either side of a robbery being reported.

The alehouses themselves were believed to be nurseries for criminals, and the constable and justices waged a constant war on unlicensed premises. The justices had been empowered to "put away" alehouses that they disapproved of, and to demand sureties for good behaviour from those they allowed to remain open. A system of licensing was implemented, and Acts under James I forbade tippling at inns by any but bona fide travellers, lodgers and working men during their lunch break. The Act of 1606 began "Whereas the loathsome and odious sin of drunkenness is of late grown into common use in this realm, being the root and foundation of many other enormous sins, as bloodshed, stabbing, murder, swearing, fornication, adultery and such like..." The fine for drunkenness was 3s. 4d., or four hours in the stocks. For keeping an unlicensed alehouse the penalty was a fine of 21s. or a whipping. Phillipa Chaunsie was keeping an unlicensed alehouse in Gilston in 1588; whether she was fined or whipped is not recorded. Thomas Draper of Hitchin went one better - in 1602 he was indicted for operating an unlicensed brewery.

In extreme cases the populace approached the justices to get alehouses closed. A petition of 1603 exists from the inhabitants of Tunford, near Cheshunt, against Robert Trimmer. It says that he is not a fit man to keep a victualling house, as he was suspected to be "infected with an unwholesome decease, as may be discovered by his speech, his hands and other parts of his body; that his wife is a notorious slut, and not fit to keep vittelinge." His wife's daughter is "a common naughtie-pack, [who] hath had one bastard and is now forward with another." Trimmer is "a common lodger of all baggage people, as rogues, tinkers, pedlars and such like and cares not whom he receives... nor from whence they come, so as he makes gain of them."

Nonetheless, unlicensed alehouses proliferated, and in 1624 Hertford Assizes were told that there were more than 540 in this county alone.

Until the second half of the 17th century, the King was held to be above the law. He could dismiss justices, and pardon offenders on a whim. James I had interfered with the judiciary, and the wrangling between Charles I and Parliament led to the Civil War of 1642-51.

Charles's execution and the Commonwealth led to the ascendancy of a puritan administration, but the puritan star had been rising for some time. From the start of the century its influence was visible in a number of measures. In 1606 an "Act to Restrain Abuses of Players" was passed, which provided that if "any person... doe... in any Stage play, Interlude, Shewe, Maygame or Pageant jestingly or prophanely speake or use the name of God or of Christ Jesus, or of the Holy Ghoste or of the Trinitie...they shall forfeite for every such Offence...Tenne Pounds." In 1623 a further act prohibited cursing or swearing by the use of the word "God," with a penalty of one shilling to the use of the poor for each oath or curse. If the offender was unwilling or unable to pay, he would be set in the stocks (if under 12, he got a whipping instead). George Carpenter of Hatfield was fined 40s. for "swearing 40 oaths," and Philip Dugard of Bishop's Stortford was set in the stocks for two oaths when he could not pay the fine. John Doggett of Tewin was fined for swearing four oaths, including the intriguing "By God he shot your dogs," and "God damme, you may kiss my wife." It is from this period that such oaths as "strewth" (God's truth) and "zounds" (God's wounds) originate, in an attempt to avoid the fine. Pagan gods were invoked - "by Jove," and "by Jupiter" became popular in this period.

Under Cromwell as Lord Protector a quartermaster found guilty of uttering impious expressions was "condemned to have his tongue bored with a red-hot iron, his sword broken over his head, and be ignominiously dismissed the service."

There was a crackdown on prostitution. Fornicators were punished by three months in gaol before being released on bail for good behaviour. Bawds risked being whipped, pilloried, branded and gaoled for up to three years. On a second offence the courts could pass a death sentence.

Restrictions were placed on the numbers and location of alehouses, and freedom of worship. The Sabbath observance laws forbade the sale of goods on Sunday. John Founch of Hemel Hempstead was prosecuted for selling shoes, and he was a parish constable at the time! Games were prohibited on the Lord's Day on pain of a 5s. fine or three hours in the stocks. Parents of children indulging in prohibited games could be fined 1s. Working on the Sabbath was also illegal - John Phipp of Stondon was summoned for grinding malt on a Sunday, as was Richard Barnard of Datchworth for travelling with his horse and cart.

In 1656 the justices of Hertfordshire were warned to watch for inn-keepers who permitted "swearing, drunkenness... tippling, gaming, or playing at Tables, Billiard Table, Shovel-board, Cards, Dice, Ninepins, Pigeon-holes, Trunks or of keeping Bowling Alley or Bowling Green... or of any other games."

With the Restoration of the crown to Charles II in 1660 came religious oppression of non-Anglicans. Four acts were passed, jointly referred to as the Clarendon Code, between 1661 and 1665. Amongst the provisions were enforced use of the Book of Common Prayer, and the prohibition of religious worship in non-Anglican form for gatherings of more than four people, unless they were of the same family.

Formed as the Society of Friends, and founded in the 1640's by George Fox, the Quakers became one of the chief targets of the courts. Hertford had been a centre for Quakers for some years. Following the Conventicle Act of 1664 prosecutions were common. Violence was often used by the constables during the arrests, and fines were heavy - often as much as £100. Nor were convictions confined to the county town. In 1668, "Thomas Gladwin, senior, of Stortford, labourer, John Reade, of the same, locksmith, William Wright of the same, tailor, Thomas Gladwin, junior, of the same, edgetool smith, Edward Herridge, of the same, tailor, Reynold Ramsey, of the same, chairmaker, John Westfield, of the same, shoemaker, & Mary Payne, of the same, spinster, all over 18 years of age, for assembling at the house of William Wright, in the parish of Stortford, with seven other unknown persons, besides the family of William Wright," were convicted for "practising a religion contrary to that set down in the liturgy."

One of the more unusual cases must be that of seven Hertford Quakers, sentenced to seven years transportation to the West Indies (the Act provided for transportation on a third conviction). Initially there was difficulty with Thomas May, the captain of their ship, the *Anne,* of London. He felt that it may be unlucky to carry the Quakers, but they were slipped aboard while he was ashore. May eventually agreed to take them at a fee of £5 each for those going to Barbados, and £6 for those with a destination of Jamaica, and the *Anne* sailed on 1st October.

The vessel suffered setback after setback as it attempted to round the North Foreland into the Channel. Other ships passed her by as the *Anne* struggled to make progress. The crew grew more and more superstitious about the Quakers, and finally the captain put them ashore at Deal in Kent on 10th November. He provided them with a letter of explanation stating that neither he nor his crew were prepared to continue the voyage with them aboard. They returned to Hertford, where they were re-arrested. Their sentence was modified to a fine of £100 each.

The Conventicle Act remained in force until 1689, but both the number and ferocity of the prosecutions fell off towards the end of that time. To his credit, Charles II had tried to repeal by royal prerogative the "penal laws in matters ecclesiastical," but he was overridden by parliament.

The same Lord Clarendon that gave his name to the Clarendon Code was also responsible in part for another important piece of legislation, but this time as a result of his abuses. He had become notorious for false imprisonment, even sending captives overseas if it served his purpose. He was impeached in 1679, and it was this, together with the refusal of some justices to issue writs during vacations, that prompted the *Habeas Corpus* Act of that year.

Habeas corpus and its predecessors had existed for hundreds of years, but now the issue of writs was put on a formal basis. Sheriffs and gaolers were given strict timescales for the production in court of the prisoner named in the writ. If in time of vacation, the Lord Chancellor had to issue a writ in his role as a justice. Those freed under a writ could not normally be re-arrested on the same charge. And no one could be imprisoned overseas (except transportees). Harsh penalties accompanied the legislation. Any judge who delayed a writ of *habeas corpus* faced forfeiting the enormous sum of £500 to the aggrieved party. If held overseas the plaintiff was entitled to sue for treble costs, with a minimum of £500.

Following Charles's death in 1685, his brother James II came to the throne with every advantage. With amazing skill he managed to throw it all away in three years, and in doing so prompted the Bill of Rights, which finished any real power of the monarchy in Great Britain forever.

James was an ardent Catholic. He was not satisfied with restoration of the rights of the followers of his religion, but took every opportunity to place them in positions of power. He seemed almost to go out of his way to antagonise those upon whose support he depended. The combination of the arrest of several senior clerics, including the Archbishop of Canterbury, coupled with the birth of a son and the consequent threat of a Catholic succession, was too much for the Commons. Several of his key supporters deserted him, and in 1688 he fled to France, which was interpreted by Parliament as an act of abdication. The throne was offered to his daughter Mary and her husband William, both Protestants, and they became joint sovereigns in 1689 after acceptance of the Bill of Rights, which must rank as one of the most important documents in the British constitution.

The Bill began with a list of what Parliament perceived as James's abuses of power:

- assuming and exercising the power of dispensing with and suspending laws.
- imprisoning and prosecuting worthy prelates (the Archbishop of Canterbury and his colleagues).
- raising and keeping a standing army within the realm.
- causing Protestants subjects to be disarmed, whilst Catholics retain their weapons.
- abuse of the jury system.
- levying of excessive bail, and imposing illegal and cruel punishments.

The second part of the bill is a declaration of the illegality of these acts, and recognition of the supremacy of parliament. The sovereign was now subservient to both parliament and the courts of law.

One of the first pieces of legislation of William and Mary's reign was the Toleration Act, which permitted all forms of Christian worship (except Unitarianism).

From 1700 to the 20th Century

Over the next two hundred and fifty years the trend towards constant legislation continued, and even today shows no sign of abating.

The violence and brutality of the 18th century gradually gave way in the 19th century to a more enlightened attitude, though progress was grudging, and gained at the expense of many setbacks.

Changes in the criminal law tended then, as now, to be reactive; legislation being passed to address problems as they arose, whether they be real or perceived. This approach is akin to treating the symptom and ignoring the disease. The predictable result is a patchwork of laws, sometimes contradictory, growing ever more complicated.

Legislation became more and more specific, and more and more verbose. Compare the following similar laws: first, King Ine of Wessex in 690 AD:

"If any one sell his own countryman, bond or free, though he be guilty, over sea, let him pay according to his wer."

Now an extract from chapter 12 of the Habeas Corpus Act of 1679:

"...and for preventing illegal imprisonments in prisons beyond the seas; be it further enacted by the authority aforesaid, that no subject of the realm that now is, or hereafter shall be an inhabitant or resident of this Kingdom of England, Dominion of Wales or Town of Berwick upon Tweed, shall or may be sent prisoner into Scotland, Ireland, Jersey, Guernsey, Tangier or into other parts, garrisons or islands or places beyond the seas, which are or at any time hereafter shall be within or without the dominions of his Majesty, his heirs or successors; and that every such imprisonment is hereby enacted and adjudged illegal; and that if any of the said subjects now is or hereafter shall be so imprisoned, shall and may for every such imprisonment maintain by virtue of this act an action or actions of false imprisonment, in any of his Majesty's courts of record, against the person or persons by whom he or she shall be so committed, detained, imprisoned, sent prisoner or transported, contrary to the true meaning of this act, and against all or any person or persons that shall frame, contrive, write, seal or countersign any warrant or writing for such commitment, detainer, imprisonment, or transportation, or shall be advising, aiding or assisting in the same, or any of them; and the plaintiff in every such action shall have judgement to recover his treble costs, besides damages, which damages so to be given, shall not be less than five hundred pounds..." and so on.

Punishments for the first half of this period were severe, with sentences ranging from fines to corporal and capital punishment for relatively minor offences. There was inconsistency between courts, and the offender's sentence was a lottery, based upon the enlightenment (or otherwise) of the presiding justices.

The criminal offence of witchcraft was repealed in 1736. Prosecutions under the act had been uncommon for some years, and Hertfordshire has the dubious honour of having passed the last death sentence for witchcraft in the country, in 1712. Jane Wenham, of Walkern, was accused of bewitching Matthew Gilson, Anne Thorne and Anne Street. Witnesses for the prosecution included two local parsons, the Reverends Gardiner and Strutt.

At Hertford Assizes on 4th March 1712, Jane was accused of covenanting with the devil. The Grand Jury swore a true bill, and the trial began before Mr. Justice Powell. The court was packed.

Amongst the evidence produced was Jane's inability to say the Lord's Prayer correctly – a sure sign of guilt to many. Instead of saying "lead us not into temptation," Jane said "lead us not into no temptation." A common dialect variation was being used as evidence in a capital trial.

After two hours the jury returned a verdict of guilty of "conversing with the devil in the shape of a cat." The judge had no option but to sentence her to death, but he suspended execution until for the time being. It was at this point that it became clear how lucky Jane was to have Mr. Justice Powell as her judge. He was a sceptic, and, with Colonel Plumer and Earl Cowper, obtained for her a royal pardon. First Plumer, and on his death, Lord Cowper, provided a home for Jane until her death in 1730. After the trial Jane said that one of the two parsons had a grudge against her because she had jilted him years before.

That was not the end of witchcraft, the law and Hertfordshire however. In 1751 an alleged witch, Ruth Osborne, died whilst being "swum" at Tring.

To an extent there was a failure by the authorities to intervene at an early stage. That Ruth and her husband John were to be swum had been advertised in several towns locally, but no action was taken.

The incident caused an outcry, in part due to the barbarity of the behaviour of some of the mob. Despite attempts to hide the couple – she was aged 70, he was a mere 56 – the threat of arson resulted in them being handed over.

The ringleader of the crowd, Thomas Colley, a chimney sweep, was reported in detail in the *Gentleman's Magazine* (though with a number of inaccuracies), as well as the newspapers.

Above: "swimming" a suspected witch. (from a contemporary print)

Law and Disorder in Hertfordshire

Great efforts were made to ensure that the culprits were brought to justice, and indeed a number of people were arrested. Only one came to trial: Thomas Colley. Found guilty, he was sentenced to be hanged and gibbeted, and the sentence was duly executed on August 23, 1751.

As the 18th century wore on, more and more offences were added to the list of capital crimes. In 1727 there were 50. By 1819 there were 241, of which 176 were without benefit of clergy. These figures are frequently referred to without qualification, but they can be deceptive. It is certainly true that for a hundred years from 1700 punishment in the courts was brutal, but no more so than in the past. It is important also to bear in mind several points:

- where benefit of clergy was available, it was regularly used to obtain what amounted to acquittal.
- juries frequently chose not to convict, even though the accused was clearly guilty.
- the value placed upon goods was heavily reduced in indictments to lighten the penalty. Stolen goods were valued at 10d. so that the offence was petty rather than grand larceny. This principle was referred to by Bracton as early as the 13th century, the intention at that time being to compensate for change in value of money.
- even if sentenced to death at Assizes, the sentence could be, and often was, commuted to transportation or imprisonment.
- many of the capital offences were closely related. There were for example 35 different types of forgery, each counting as a capital offence.
- a woman with child might "plead her belly" to obtain a reprieve, though quite obviously this could be for no more than nine months.

The result was that executions were less common than one might think, and in only about twenty-five of those technically capital offences was the death penalty actually applied. London and Middlesex combined only managed an average of 35 executions per annum between 1775 and 1800. The national average between 1805 and 1820 was about 76. Of the 2,218 capital convictions for that period, less than 40% were executed.

Nonetheless, capital punishment was a lottery, and executions took place that both surprised and shocked the community. John Carrington recorded in his diary for 9th March 1807 that "John Catheral Hanged at Hartford Fryday 20th for Poarching or Snearing and for Resisting the Constable...which Sentance too Bad."

The large number of offences carrying the death sentence must have made it difficult for the felon to be sure of just where he stood. Larceny, for example, could be a capital offence depending upon where, when, and how the theft took place, and the value of the stolen goods. Even whether the thief wore a disguise, or whether the victim knew the offence was taking place, could make a difference. For example, the death penalty was available for the following offences:

- theft of goods worth more than 5 shillings, privately from a shop or stable.
- theft of goods from a dwelling house worth more than 40 shillings.
- theft of money or goods from the person worth more than 12d.

Attempts from 1808 onwards to reduce the sentence for the theft of goods worth more than 5 shillings were defeated several times in the House of Lords.

Perhaps just as shocking were some the non-capital sentences handed down:

1589	Judith Bibstone, stealing cloth. Guilty, value 10d., whipped.
1674	William Bassill of Hertford, for killing and taking away a red deer from the wood or the close of James, Earl of Salisbury. Six months in the house of correction. He was lucky - his sentence could easily have been more severe.
1699	"Mary Thomas, spinster, taken... in an unlicensed alehouse of ill repute...known as loose and disorderly..." *Pending legal process* (my italics) she was to be punished by whipping and hard labour.
1774	Elizabeth Parr, theft of nutmeg in Hitchin: public whipping and three months in the house of correction.
1785	John Harding, committed to the house of correction for 12 months for being "an incorrigible rogue."
1820	William Reed, for dishonestly obtaining a cheese worth 20 shillings, imprisoned for six months in St. Albans Borough Gaol.
1827	George Bates, £2 or two months' imprisonment for "having on 20 Dec last stolen and taken away in the parish of Hemel Hempstead the top of an Ornamental Holly Tree the property of E. J. Calcott Esq."

It is worth noting that most of these offences are against property. Those that made the law were predominantly from the wealthier sections of society, and were deeply concerned with protecting the status quo.

Offences against the person were treated more lightly than they are today. Consider the following sentences:

1769	a pretended clergyman, for attempting to rape a child under 10

years of age, received six months imprisonment and two spells in the pillory, and fined security for good behaviour for one year.

1770   attempted ravishment of Sarah Hilyard by Samuel Harris, fined 6s. 8d.

1789   assault on Thomas Everstaff by James Cummins, fined 6d.

1828   Joseph Burgess fined £2, or one month's imprisonment at Hertford, for having "on this 24th day of December at the parish of Flamstead assaulted and beat John Taylor."

Sentences became progressively more humane as the nineteenth century progressed. The decline in severity was not an overnight affair, but a slow process, as the authorities realised that Jeremy Bentham and other reformers had been right when they pointed out that savage penalties did not deter the criminal. If they did, crime rates should be falling, and they were not. In fact there was reason to believe that offenders were actually being acquitted because the penalties were so heavy: juries were unwilling to convict a man for theft and risk him being hanged. In 1808 Sir Samuel Romilly convinced Parliament that this was exactly what was happening, and picking pockets was removed from the capital list. A Commons Select Committee in 1816 heard that the number of convictions had indeed risen in consequence.

The reformers argued that what was needed was certainty of capture, coupled with the reformation of the prisoner. Until offenders really believed they would be caught, most would convince themselves that they would not. Of course, none of this applied to crimes committed in the heat of the moment, when no thought is given to the outcome of one's actions.

By the mid 19th century, capital punishment was reserved for the most serious of offences. At the end of the century only treason, murder, and offences under the Piracy Act of 1837 and the Dockyard Protection Act of 1772 were left. Sentences were still harsh, however, and despite the almost universal belief that a man is innocent until proven guilty, there were offences where the accused had to prove his innocence. Anyone caught with dead game could go to prison for two months unless he could show that he came by it lawfully; and anyone apprehended within 20 miles of Charing Cross with property that might reasonably be considered stolen could receive a similar sentence unless he could satisfactorily account for the goods.

As the use of capital and corporal punishment declined up to the middle of the 19th century, the courts relied more on imprisonment, in most cases for relatively short terms. The result was overcrowding, and it became clear from the number of repeat offenders that imprisonment was not working as a deterrent either. In 1895, the rate of re-committal for larceny was 78%. Alternatives to prison were needed, ones that reduced the number of re-offenders.

The Probation of First Offenders Act of 1887 was a success, though whether the figure of only 10% of those sentenced under the act re-offending or breaking the terms of their probation in years 1897-99 is accurate is questionable. In order to reduce the number of prisoners on remand, the Bail Act of 1898 gave magistrates the power to release offenders on bail without sureties, provided they were convinced that this would not defeat the ends of justice. The introduction of payment of fines by instalments in the Criminal Justice Administration Act of 1914 helped reduce the number of committals for petty offences. The same act empowered the police to release prisoners on bail.

Until the mid 19th century youth was no defence against a harsh sentence. Ann Mead was only fourteen when she hanged at Hertford in 1800, though her crime was not a pleasant one; she was convicted of poisoning with arsenic one of the children, aged 1½, of her employer, a Mr. Proctor of Royston. The motive seems to have been revenge, following an argument with Mrs. Proctor during which Ann was referred to as "a slut." William Lawrence of Great Hormead was 10 when he was prosecuted for breaking into the house of Ezekiel Elliott in 1815 and stealing a handkerchief and a watch. He was transported to Australia for seven years, as was Robert Euston of Cheshunt, aged 12, for stealing from the person 4 sovereigns, a £1 note and 9 shillings in silver in 1826. (It has been alleged that the youngest prison inmate in the 19th century was only three, charged with contempt before the Court of Chancery of the Duchy of Lancaster). Young offenders were placed in the same gaols as habitual criminals, where they learned criminal attitudes and techniques. The effect was to increase crime rather than reduce it.

Concern for the youth of the nation was growing, however, both for young offenders and young victims. From 1st July 1842 it became an offence to allow a person under 21 years of age to "ascend or descend a Chimney, or enter a Flue, for the purpose of sweeping, cleaning or coring the same, or for extinguishing fire therein." The penalty was a fine of between £5 and £10. In default of payment, imprisonment "in Common Gaol or House of Correction, with or without Hard Labour, as the Justices shall seem meet, for any time not exceeding Two Calendar Months." Nonetheless, in 1899 the Hertfordshire Constable's Handbook drew attention to this offence, so it presumably still occurred. Books by Henry Mayhew and his collaborators described the lifestyles of the London poor, including children, and Dickens' novels did the same; the result was an upswell of public sympathy.

Law and Disorder in Hertfordshire

The Youthful Offenders Act of 1854 recommended that children should go to reformatory schools rather than gaols. By the end of 1857, 45 schools had been established. Thirty-four were for boys, and ten for girls. One was mixed.

Sir William Harcourt, Home Secretary from 1880-85, was concerned about the number of young offenders in gaol, and sought to reduce their sentences (Queen Victoria was recorded as saying she thought they should be whipped).

1908 was a year of major reform in respect of young offenders. Imprisonment of children and young persons was abolished, as was capital punishment for offenders under eighteen. Juvenile Courts with specialist magistrates were established. All these measures were under the Children's Act. In that year too the Borstal institutions were established. The age group 16-21 had been recognised as that in which most habitual criminal behaviour was formed, and the Borstals targeted it, with the emphasis on reform.

The second quarter of the 19th century had brought the railway to Hertfordshire, and with it two further sources of crime, one old, one new. The navvies that laid the tracks were an unruly bunch, and theft, poaching, violence and drunkenness followed their progress. Some residents even left the area when they heard that the railway was coming through - this had happened before with the construction of the canal system, and they knew what to expect. What was new was the advantage the new form of transport provided to the Metropolitan criminal. He need only travel a few miles and he was in an area where he was unknown, and an area of comparatively unsophisticated crime control at that.

In London in the early 1860's a spate of robberies occurred, in which the victim was half strangled by one assailant whilst another rifled his pockets. A third member of the gang kept watch. These robberies were followed by copycat offences throughout the country. In part the sensational press reports were responsible for the spread. The number of capital sentences the courts handed down for other crimes increased as the courts reacted. The Government too felt obliged to respond, and as a knee-jerk reaction they passed the "Garotters' Act," reintroducing flogging for such crimes.

With the rise of this form of violent theft there was a corresponding fall in the far more skilful art of picking pockets, though the fall in the popularity of the coat-tail amongst fashionable gentlemen, a favourite target of the pickpocket, may also have contributed to its decline.

The Habitual Criminals Act of 1869 required descriptions of all such offenders to be held centrally in London. In some cases the new science of photography was used, and some of these early photographs are very poignant. The example below is from Cambridgeshire.

Right: Mary Ann Barber, aged 12. She stole a hat and a pair of boots, and got 1 month hard labour followed by five years in a reformatory school. (Cambridgeshire Constabulary Archives).

Until the closing years of the 19th century, the view taken by authority was that each person was responsible for his or her actions, with a choice of whether to commit an offence or not. The offender chose his life of crime. The consequence was that extenuating circumstances were not often taken into account in sentencing, though the capacity in law to do so was there. The object of the sentence was "suffering, inflicted as a punishment for crime, and the fear of repetition of it." The criminal opted to commit the offence, now he must suffer his just desserts.

Certain trends continued into the 20th century, but efforts to understand the offender and his motivation, and reforming his character, began. Some took the view that the emphasis on the offender went too far, to the detriment of the victim.

The trend away from harsh punishment for property crime was also sustained, whilst some crimes against the person (for example rape) were more heavily punished than in the past. Where possible imprisonment became the option of last resort, and fines, probation and cautions were used more frequently.

William I had abolished capital punishment; Henry II reintroduced it. After more than 800 years, it was abandoned for a second time in the early 1960's. Dire warnings of an orgy of killing notwithstanding, there was not an immediate escalation in offences of murder. The call for reintroduction of the death penalty followed a number of high profile killings, usually with the already discredited claim that it acted as a deterrent.

Crime figures regularly showed an increase, but this was in part due to the increasing number of offences created by government, and an increasing willingness of the public to report offences.

Succeeding governments failed to learn from past experience that panic legislation under pressure from the press rarely makes good law, and knee-jerk legislation continued, and continues, to be enacted.

Some Interesting and Unusual Laws and Offences

Sheepskin Shields
Under the laws of King Aethelstan in the 10th century, the use of sheepskin in the construction of shields was forbidden, on pain of a fine of 30 shillings. The reason seems to have been that sheepskin is an inferior leather for this purpose.

Escaped Anglo-Saxon Slaves
Ine, King of Wessex, in about 690 AD, decreed that "if any one go from his lord without leave, or steal himself away into another shire, and he be discovered, let him go where he was before, and pay to his lord 60s." The intention was to deter escaping slaves. If however the escapee could get to a borough, and live there without being reclaimed for a year and a day, he became a free man.

The Forest Laws
There were a number of royal forests, the purpose of which was to provide hunting for the royal household. On the borders of Hertfordshire are Waltham Forest and Epping Forest.

Their origins are Anglo-Saxon, but their importance grew under the Normans. William I and his son, William Rufus, were both avid hunters. Henry I further extended the laws concerning the forests, and after some slight relaxation under Stephen, they were substantially reiterated by Henry II. The punishments were made slightly less severe, but were enforced with greater rigour. As a serious bone of contention with the barons in 1215, the laws were addressed in Magna Carta. Charles I revived the forest laws in an attempt to raise revenue, but they were finally swept away by parliament in 1640.

In these royal forests different laws applied from the rest of the country. Forest Courts - the Swainmote, and the Woodmote - tried suits and transgressors.

Anyone could own land within the forest, but they were subject to strict regulation. No fence was to be so high as to be uncrossable by a deer with her fawn; farmers could not drive deer from their crops; and new buildings required permission, for fear that an increase in the human population might frighten the deer. The king's men could cut branches from anyone's trees to provide winter feed. All dogs had to have three claws clipped, to prevent them chasing deer.

The penalties for transgressors were severe, being death or mutilation. The accused might have a long wait to know his fate, as sentences were only delivered once in every three years.

Suicide

Suicide, as an offence against God, was illegal for centuries, at least since medieval times. But how can you punish suicide?

If a person took his or her own life deliberately, they were said to have done so *felo de se,* and their property was subject to confiscation. (*Felo* = felon, *de* = of, *se* = oneself; thus, committing a felony against oneself). An example occurred at Clopton, a village long abandoned near Croydon, just over the border in Cambridgeshire. In 1260 Lawrence of Clopton was found hanged in the barn of Peter the tailor by John de Novelhorne. The verdict was *felo de se*, and his chattels to the value of 45s. 4½d. were forfeit to the crown. (Part of the village is now a field, where it is still possible to make out the sites of roads and buildings).

Nicholas Johnson of Coles Hill, a yeoman, was indicted for suicide at Hertford Assizes in 1610. On 21 December the year before he had hanged himself in his barn with a halter (value 1d).

The word *suicide* was originally reserved for those of unsound mind. The indictment for that offence, not *felo de se*, would have preserved his estate for those he left behind.

Much later attempted suicides were remanded in prison to receive the advice of the prison chaplain. In the 19th century there were more women than men in prison for the offence, though usually more men than women try to kill themselves.

The methods most favoured by suicides have varied over the years. In the St. Albans Borough Quarter Sessions Rolls for the period 1784 - 1820 there are seven suicides referred to; three hangings, three cut throats and one poisoning. With the introduction of gas in the first half of 19th century came a new and painless method, and by 1936 it was the most popular in Britain, used by nearly 35% of suicides. (In the USA firearms were most commonly used at 37%; in Germany 53.7% of suicides opted for hanging).

In more recent times, suicide could invalidate life assurance policies, and there was a stigma attached to the deed. For these reasons, for many years coroner's courts have adopted the practice where possible of avoiding a verdict of suicide.

Suicide ceased to be a criminal offence in 1961.

Law and Disorder in Hertfordshire

Sex and the Law

Most sexual offences were the domain of Ecclesiastical Courts until the 16th century. They had no power to inflict physical punishment upon offenders, and the majority of penalties consisted of penance or excommunication. The penances were based on the principle of fasting and abstinence from sexual activity, and were listed in documents called penitentials.

Punishment depended upon age, marital status, and profession. The more mature person, who presumably should have known better than to offend, was punished more heavily than the young; the married more than the single; and the cleric more than the layman. Fornication between two unmarried people carried one or two years' penance (unless with a serving girl, in which case the sentence was halved). For male masturbation by the hand the penitentials listed ten days penance; if you used a piece of wood, the penance was doubled. Almost every sexual practice was covered.

Henry II regulated prostitution in Southwark. Brothels were not to open on holy days. This must have damaged their trade, as there were more than one hundred and fifty holy days in the 12th century. Days when parliament was sitting were also banned. Pregnant women were not to ply their trade, nor married women or nuns. And girls were not to charge unless they had spent the whole night with their customer.

There followed several anti-prostitution campaigns during the reigns of Edward I, Edward III, Henry V, and somewhat surprisingly, in 1546, Henry VIII, though venereal disease had reached serious proportions at that time, which might explain his concern. The penalty was to be carried through the parish in a cart, with a notice upon the front or back of the offender's dress proclaiming her trade.

There were purges by the puritans in the following century. Fornication was punishable by three months in gaol, followed by being bound over for good behaviour. "Bawds" were condemned to be whipped, pilloried, branded and gaoled for up to three years; a second conviction could result in a capital sentence.

The Contagious Diseases Prevention Act of 1864 made a medical examination of all girls working close to eleven of England's garrison towns compulsory. If they were found to be carrying a sexually transmitted disease, they were forcibly detained in hospital, in order to stop them infecting servicemen. Five years later, the legislation was extended to include a further seven towns. A campaign to have the law repealed began, but two separate reports favoured retention. Nonetheless, in 1883 the House of Commons passed a resolution condemning the forcible medical examination of women, and as the resolution included a refusal to pay for such examinations, the practice was dropped. The law was repealed in 1886.

Until 1875, the age of sexual consent for girls was 12 (for boys it was 14). It was raised to 13, and ten years later the Criminal Law Amendment Act of 1885 made it a felony to have sex with a girl under 13. It was however only a misdemeanour if she was aged between 13 and 16. The same act made procuration an offence.

Though unconnected with sexual offences but interesting nonetheless, until 1925 there was an assumption in law that if a woman committed an offence in the presence of her husband, she did so under his coercion.

Archery

The longbow was for many years the most important weapon in England's arsenal. Its effective use required training, strength and practice, and when other sports caught the Englishman's fancy something had to be done. From the 14th century the authorities did all they could to ensure that all Englishmen became skilled archers. Edward III expressed concern that archery practice was being neglected. Richard II and Henry VI legislated that on Sundays and holydays all men strong and able of body were to use their bows and arrows, and 'utterly to leave playing at the balls, as well as hond-ball and foot-ball, and other games called quoits, dice, bowling and kails...' (kails, or kayles, was a form of ninepins imported from France).

'The myghte of the realme stode upon archers,' and those who did not practise on Sundays and Feast-days were in trouble with the law. Under a statute of Edward IV, a fine of one halfpenny was levied against those who failed to comply.

In 1472, Venetian merchants importing wine into England had to supply 'four good bowstaves' per butt of wine, or face a fine of 6s. 8d. In 1483 Richard III increased the number of bowstaves to twelve, and the fine to 13s. 4d.

In 1502 the duty on bowstaves over 6 ft. in length was abolished, in order to encourage the use of powerful bows. The price of a bow was already restricted to a maximum of 3s. 4d., with a fine of 20s. for default.

From 1465 butts were established throughout the country by statute, and their existence remains in place-names throughout the country. Examples in Hertfordshire included the Buttfield at Berkhamsted, Colney Butts in Watford, Butts Close in Hitchin and Butt Field View in St. Albans. They were extended to the new statutory range of 220 yards in 1541. The same act of Henry VII refers to the crossbow, hagbut, and demi-hake (the latter two being early types of firearm) causing the 'good and laudable exercise of the long-bow' to be neglected.

In 1515 Henry VIII forbade the use of 'crosebow nor handgon except he haue possessyons to the yerely valew of ccc. marke (£200) or els lycence from hensforth by the kynges placard.' It was an offence to have a crossbow or gun in the house, except for those who made or dealt in them, and the inhabitants of walled towns within seven miles of the sea. Crossbows were also permitted for self defence against the Scots.

Amongst his many other duties, the parish constable was responsible for the maintenance of the butts, or targets, for the archers, and for ensuring that able-bodied men practised as required.

It was a losing battle. Early firearms were less effective than a properly used longbow. They were slower to load, less accurate and usually less powerful. But they had one crucial advantage - they required relatively little training. It took years to become proficient in the use of the longbow. An army could be formed much more quickly if it was armed with guns. By the end of the 16th century the bow had become almost obsolete as a weapon of war.

Rook Law

In 1532 it was made obligatory for the population to kill as many rooks and crows as they could. Every township, parish, hamlet, borough or village had to provide, at its own cost, a crow net, which had to be kept in good repair. The rate paid to those licensed to capture the birds was 2d. each.

The reason behind the purge was the damage the birds were doing to crops and to thatch. The fine for non-compliance was 10s., but spread across the community the cost was relatively small. This may be why the villages of Great and Little Wymondley managed to break the law and incur the fine twice at least, in 1575 and 1606.

Wear a Cap! 1570

"Every person over seven years of age shall wear upon Sabbath or holy days upon their head, a cap of wool, knit, thicked and dressed in England, made within this realm and only dressed and finished by some of the trade of cappers. Forfeit for every day of not wearing, 3s. 4d. Except maids, ladies, gentlemen, noble personages and every lord, knight and gentleman of twenty marks land and their heirs and such as have borne office of worship of any city..."

The purpose of the legislation, repealed in 1597, was the protection of the cloth industry. The fine is substantial, so this was a law to be taken seriously. It was

The Resurrection Men, or Bodysnatchers

Bodysnatching became common in the first quarter of the nineteenth century. The trade catered for the demands of the schools of anatomy, and the "resurrection men" haunted the graveyards following funerals. A fresh corpse could fetch as much as £9. Iron coffins and railings (mortsafes) were brought into use. Edward Bridgeman advertised wrought-iron coffins: "many hundred dead bodies will be dragged from their wooden coffins this winter" he claimed in Wooler's British Gazette in 1822. Churchyards erected gates to protect the dead, and the bereaved paid watchers (sometimes armed) to care for their loved ones until decomposition made the body worthless. Mr. J. M. Reade was paid 30 shillings for watching the grave of Mrs. Cross in the churchyard of South Mimms for twelve nights, and Louisa Arrowsmith's diary records that the family vault was watched for several days after an interment.

From the time of Henry VIII, the bodies of four executed prisoners had been given to the medical profession each year for research. From 1726, all executed criminals were supposed to be handed over. (After her execution for murder in Hertford in 1800, fourteen year old Ann Mead's body was given to a medical man, Dr. Bradley, for dissection).

But supply clearly did not meet demand. It was only in the eighteenth century that surgeons split from barbers – before then, you went to the same man for a haircut or an amputation. By 1810 there were almost two thousand medical students in London and Edinburgh alone, and only about 76 executions a year. Bodies were shipped in from the Continent; they were claimed from hospitals and workhouses by bogus relatives; some were even murdered by the likes of Burke and Hare in Edinburgh; but mostly they were stolen from their graves.

Above: a mortsafe surrounding the Cathrow family vault, in the churchyard at Great Amwell. Dating from the late 1820's, it is intended to deter bodysnatchers. Grave watchers were often employed as well. (author)

The Royal College of Surgeons has in its records the diary of a bodysnatcher. A single entry is enough to give a flavour of its contents:

"Friday, 28th February 1812: Met at Jack Got 4 large (adults) 1 small (a child) and 1 Foetus, Harps [the name of the graveyard]. Took them to London."

A Parliamentary Select Committee was set up to investigate the trade in 1828. They heard that one London gang in one winter alone had stolen 312 bodies, netting well over £1,000. It was the bodies of the poor that were most at risk, said one resurrection man; they were not buried as deeply as the wealthy.

The solution the Committee recommended was that executed criminals should no longer be "anatomized." The supply of bodies should come from the workhouses and poorhouses, where the previous year over 3,000 people had been buried at the expense of the taxpayer. At one in three of these interments, no relatives had attended the funeral at all.

In March 1829 a "Bill for preventing the unlawful disinterment of human bodies, and for regulating Schools of Anatomy" was thrown out by the House of Lords. Only three years later the Select Committee's recommendations became law, following another murder in order to supply the surgeons (by now known as "Burking"). The Anatomy Act of 1832 required schools to apply for a licence, and grave robbing was made a misdemeanour punishable by a fine or imprisonment. The practice continued for some time after that however - in 1839 John Aley was employed by Thomas Smith of Little Hadham to fetch the body of his son from Bishop's Stortford. It had been stolen after burial in Little Hadham churchyard. Aley collected the body from the constables and brought it back, where William had the unpleasant task of identifying his son for a second time.

Finally, Two Unusual Capital Offences:
Injuring Westminster Bridge.
Impersonating an out-pensioner of the Chelsea Hospital.

Readers with designs upon either of these bastions of the British establishment will be glad to know that neither offence still carries the death penalty.

Chapter Two

Courts and Trials

By 943 AD, the country was divided into shires, and each shire was sub-divided into hundreds. A hundred contained about a hundred tithes, hence its name. It is upon this structure that law enforcement and the Anglo-Saxon courts were based.

Each shire had an ealdorman, or alderman, who presided over a Shire Court held twice a year. In Hertfordshire it was held at Hertford. There were also Hundred Courts, which had the same jurisdiction as the Shire Court, though the latter tended to hear the more serious cases. The Hundred Courts met every four weeks. From the time of Edgar (about 960 AD) the bishop of the shire and an ealdorman sat in both these courts, and cases secular and ecclesiastical, civil and criminal were tried in them. As the judicial head of the shire, the ealdorman received one third of the fines levied by the court.

The Witenagemot could hear cases too, but only if for some reason the lower courts would not; and there was no right of appeal from this or any other Anglo-Saxon court, though the king could intervene if he saw fit to do so.

On a par with the Hundred Courts were the Borough Courts, recognised by Edgar. They met three times a year, and the borough dwellers were exempted from the Hundred Court (but not the Shire Court). By the time of the Norman invasion, these boroughs were almost self-governing, with their own by-laws and courts, and economic privileges such as fairs or restrictive trading advantages.

Manor Courts dealt with local matters. Inheritances, land transfers, and boundary disputes were grist to their mill. They also tried minor offences against the custom of the manor. Their main tool in punishing wrongdoers was the fine, but they occasionally exceeded their powers. The presiding officer was the lord of the manor or his steward, with a jury formed from the tenants. Where fines were levied, the amount was decided upon by two members of the jury, known as affreerers. When criminal offences were tried, the defendant could call upon compurgators to swear on his behalf. In Wymondley in 1333, John Grene placed himself at law six-handed (meaning he agreed to find six compurgators) in defence of a charge of theft of chickens from the vicar, Roger Maryot.

The other administrative unit as yet unmentioned was the township. It may be older than the shire and the hundred, and may have had its own court; if so, it was probably similar in power to the Manor Court.

Law and Disorder in Hertfordshire

It was possible for a manor or a lordship to be large enough to encapsulate an entire hundred, or a large part of one. Where this occurred, a charter creating a semiautonomous unit was sometimes granted by the crown. This unit, called a 'liberty, ' was independent of the hundreds, but remained part of the shire. After the Norman Conquest, the number of liberties grew.

The best-known liberty in Hertfordshire is the Liberty of St. Albans, which has remained remarkably persistent. Edward IV gave the Abbot power over all matters concerning the gaol, a privilege confirmed by Henry VII, coupled with the appointment of justices for the Liberty. Henry VIII abolished the powers of many liberties, but the Borough of St. Albans was accepted.

The principles and procedures of all these courts were similar. They fell between a primitive system of private vengeance, where the victim or his kin obtain their own justice, and the modern system, where the state is responsible for the prosecution and punishment of offenders.

In the Hundred Court the court president was the ealdorman, hundredman or sometimes the sheriff. Judgement was by the assembly or an appointed committee. In this respect these courts were similar in structure to the Anglo-Saxon folkesmotes. The president of the court had a right of veto, and pronounced the sentence. The Shire Court was similar; though following the decline in power of the ealdorman, the sheriff became the court president.

It was the responsibility of the individual to bring the prosecution before the court. He or she might also have to set the date for the trial, and if necessary, carry out the judgement of the court, even if this meant death for the offender. The state controlled the procedure of the court, no more.

There was a great deal of swearing of oaths in early trials. We must remember that this was a religious and superstitious society, and oaths were not something to take lightly - to lie under oath meant damnation for one's soul. One party or the other (usually the defendant) was 'awarded proof.' This meant that at the next session of the court he would either have to find witnesses to testify on his behalf, or enough compurgators prepared to swear that they believed him innocent. The number required was laid down by custom and law. The relative value of a man's oath was defined according to his *wer*, and his status; according to the code of Hlothhere, for example, "a twelve hundredman's oath stands for six ceorls' oaths." Proof of innocence by means of compurgators lasted for centuries. The practice was not formally repealed until 1833, though it had been out of use for many years before then.

Trial by ordeal was used most often when the court could not decide whether to award proof to the plaintiff or the accused, and decided that divine intervention was required. For some offences, ordeal was the only option by law.

The ordeal was based on the principle that God would not permit an innocent person to be found guilty, and would protect them from harm. The practice was imported from the Franks, who used it in the 6th century as a means of controlling vendettas, which were getting out of hand. Whether it is derived from earlier pagan rituals is unknown. It was in use in England by the 7th century, and references to it appear in the code of King Ine.

Contrary to popular belief, being proven innocent in trial by ordeal was not impossible, nor did it necessarily result in the death of the accused. The real thing was more reasonable, though still painful and certainly dangerous, but the accused had a chance. It is hard to believe, even in an age when the power of the church was immense, that such a manner of trial could be thought reliable; but then, a thousand years later people still believed in witches, and subjected them to similar torment.

There were four types of trial by ordeal. All were carried out under the control of the church, and would begin with a period of prayer and fasting, followed by the trial itself.

- Ordeal by fire: the accused carried a piece of red-hot iron of a defined weight a specified distance. The burned hand was then bound up and left for three days. If after that period the burn was healing cleanly, the accused was declared innocent. Depending upon the nature of the crime, the iron weighed either one or three pounds. It is sometimes claimed that any burning must disappear within three days for a "not guilty" verdict. This is a myth: clearly, if it were true, every person subjected to trial would be proven guilty. A variation used in Europe involved red-hot ploughshares.
- Ordeal of boiling water: a stone was suspended in boiling water, the depth being dependent on the gravity of the offence. The accused had to recover the stone. Thereafter the procedure was the same as for ordeal by fire.
- Ordeal of cold water: the accused was bound left hand to right foot, and right hand to left foot. Around their waist was tied a rope, with a knot at a specified distance from the body. He was then thrown into cold water, and if he sank to the depth of the knot, he was innocent. This form of ordeal survived the others as the "swimming" of suspected witches. A variant says that if the accused "began once to plunge and labour for Breath immediately upon his falling into the Liquor, he was condemn'd as guilty of the Crime, and receiv'd his Punishment for it."
- Ordeal by swallowing a consecrated substance: the accused had to swallow consecrated bread or holy water of a specified weight or volume. Failure pronounced his guilt.

Ordeal by fire was reserved for nobles and the freeborn men and women of the country. The unfree were subjected to ordeal by water. Trial by consecrated substance was probably reserved for the clergy (a cynic might think this is because it was less painful than the others).

Above: wager of battle, or trial by combat. From a thirteenth century document.

The Normans brought with them a new form of ordeal: trial by battle, also known as trial by combat or wager of battle. Initially at least this form of ordeal was not obligatory for Englishmen. There are similarities to trial by ordeal, in that it was assumed that God would influence the outcome in favour of justice. The young, the sick and the aged could claim exemption, and in certain circumstances a champion could take the place of either of the combatants. Theoretically the option of trial by battle was available to all free men, but in practice it was rarely exercised by any but the aristocracy, almost as a mark of status.

The form of the combat was strictly adhered to. The accuser and accused went through a formal challenge ceremony, and the court appointed a date for the battle. The accused was held in prison until that date, though he was well treated, and provided with adequate food and drink. On the day of the combat, the two were armed alike, with bastons not more than three feet long, with a double-headed horn beak, and square shields. They fought bare-headed and on foot, until one or the other was defeated, or until sunset. If the accused successfully defended himself until then, he was deemed innocent. Should he lose, he would be punished as guilty. A severe sentence of a year and a day's imprisonment was the punishment for any form of interference by the spectators.

A Stanstead man was involved in such a trial in 1375, the details of which are recorded in the Red Book of Colchester:

"A certain Approver, John Hubberd, of Halsted, accused one John Bokenham, of Stanstede Thele, of various robberies and homicides by them jointly committed... The said John and John, being led before the justices, and clothed in leather coats, with staves pointed with horn, and with targets (shields) in their hands, and licence being given by the justices aforesaid and licence proclaimed as the custom is, they began the terrible duel thus joined. At length the aforesaid Approver overcame the person accused, so that he acknowledged himself the culprit, saying "Criaunt, criaunt." And the self-same day the said accused was hanged, and the said Approver was led again into the aforesaid castle."

Several cases were tried by battle in Hertfordshire following the Peasants' Revolt in 1381.

Trial by ordeal was abolished in England in 1218, three years after the Lateran Council of 1215, under Pope Innocent III. Pope Alexander II had banned its use for clergy in 1063 - why he felt the rest of the population should suffer for another 150 years is unclear.

Trial by battle somehow slipped through the net, and remained legal long after other forms of trial by ordeal had disappeared. Henry Chauncy in his *Historical Antiquities of Hertfordshire*, published in 1700, mentioned that the practice was still legal; the matter came to a head in 1818 with the case of Abraham Thornton. He was accused of the murder of Mary Ashford, but there was inadequate evidence to convict him. Mary's brother invoked wager of battle. An act was passed in parliament in 1819 to repeal this rather interesting form of trial.

The penalties available to the courts were much the same as in Anglo-Saxon times. The lower courts could levy fines or order minor corporal punishment, and the superior courts could also inflict flogging, mutilation and death upon offenders.

In 1154 Henry II succeeded to the throne, and the court system went through important changes. When Henry became King, the most important courts were

> The King's Bench
> The Court of Common Pleas
> The Shire and Hundred Courts
> Manor Courts, both Baron and Leet
> Borough Courts
> Ecclesiastical Courts

Exactly when itinerant justices were sent through the shires is uncertain. There is reason to believe that both William I and Henry I had done something of the kind, but Henry II formalized the practice. Under the terms of the Assize of Clarendon in 1166 (not to be confused with the similarly named Constitutions), a commission of justices was set up to visit the shires. To these justices, and the sheriff, were to be presented 'notorious or reputed offenders.' These were the assize courts, at least in embryonic form, that were eventually to supersede the Shire and Hundred Courts. They were the means by which the King's Court - the *Curia Regis* - was brought to the provinces.

These courts and the itinerant justices are crucial to two highly important aspects of English law. As they travelled through the land, they spread a consistent version of the law, which became known as the Common Law. At the same time, based on the fact that as the King's Court, the *Curia Regis* was the supreme court, it was not itself obliged to comply with the Common Law; it could interpret the law - a principle called Equity. The upshot was that the court could dispense real justice.

Juries began to be used in lieu of ordeal, though not in the form that we know them. The jurymen were not expected to hear evidence and pronounce upon it, but rather judge the case from their own local knowledge, for which they were recruited. They were expected to declare whether they knew of any persons who had been accused, or were suspected of being a "robber, or murderer, or thief, or of being a receiver of robbers, or murderers, or thieves, since the Lord King has been King." This form of jury came to be known as the "Grand Jury."

There was an obvious flaw with this system. In many cases local men were being asked to inform on, and pronounce the guilt of, local criminals. They might be friends or neighbours. Unsurprisingly the acquittal rate was often high - the Gaol Delivery Rolls for Hertfordshire show that in the year 1324, of 285 charged, only 43 were convicted.

Compurgators were not permitted; the opinion of the jury was final, subject only to the option of trial by ordeal for the accused. When trial by ordeal was abolished, the effect on criminal trials was that indictment by the Grand Jury was tantamount to a guilty verdict (though trial by battle was still available).

Just after the middle of the 14th century a second jury, known as a 'petty' jury, of twelve men was introduced. Their responsibility was to try the case on the evidence, in much the same way that they do today.

The combination of justice and the jury system made the new courts highly popular. Though the Shire and Hundred Courts and the *Curia Regis* continued side-by-side for a while, the old system was doomed as a real power, especially when in 1278 the Statute of Gloucester placed a financial limit of 40s. on the value of cases it could try.

The *Curia Regis* used the existing court machinery - indeed, the sheriff might sit upon it as a justice. However, the sheriff's days were numbered too, and the post eventually declined from the most powerful man in the shire to little more than an executive officer of the court.

This is perhaps a good time to look at Ecclesiastical Courts. Under Anglo-Saxon rule there was no distinction between secular and church courts. William I had separated the two. He barred bishops and archdeacons from actions that might encroach upon the secular, leaving such to "the judgement of men of the world."

Stephen undid much of William's effort, and granted the church the right to try clerics in both civil and criminal matters; so that when Henry II became king, he found that a large part of the state was no longer under his control. The church punished its own, and the tendency was for those punishments to be light.

Henry attempted to re-establish the status quo from the reign of William I, and it was upon this matter he clashed most seriously with the Archbishop of Canterbury, Thomas Becket.

Their first conflict however concerned the "sheriff's aid." The sheriff of each county, as the representative of the crown, visited each hundred every year. To help with the expenses a tax called the sheriff's aid was levied, and Henry wanted this to be paid to the exchequer. Becket thwarted him in this.

More serious was the conflict over the Constitutions of Clarendon in 1164. The main bone of contention was criminous clerics; Henry wanted them tried by the lay courts, whilst Becket was anxious that ecclesiastical courts should have jurisdiction. A compromise was agreed upon, that they should be accused before the King's Court, tried by the church, and if guilty, returned to the state for punishment. Becket reneged, which brought the disapproval of even his own bishops. He fled to France, but on his return six years later he was murdered by over-zealous courtiers, in Canterbury Cathedral. Henry's contrition over the death of the man who had once been his close friend was genuine.

One of the results of the affair was the prolonging of a system known as benefit of clergy for several hundred years. As we have seen, in the 12th century it was claimed that clergy should be tried in spiritual rather than temporal courts, thus escaping the full rigours of the law. Concessions made following Becket's murder perpetuated this privilege.

In 1350 the benefit was extended to secular clerics as well. Eventually the test of a cleric became the ability to read, in Latin, psalm 51, which became known as 'the neck verse': "Have mercy upon me, O God, according to thy loving kindness: according unto the multitude of thy tender mercies blot out my transgressions." Even this requirement was abolished in 1705. Illiterate peers were included from 1547, and women, partially in 1622, and fully 70 years later.

From the late 15th century, laymen who had claimed benefit of clergy were branded on the thumb in open court, with an 'M' for manslaughter or an 'F' for felony. Benefit was thus restricted to a single crime only. Even so, this amounted to a licence to commit serious crime with impunity. The practice seems still to have been alive at least as late as 1766, when Mary Gray, or Grey, of Wideford, spinster, was convicted of theft of a stuff gown value 2s., a shift value 1s., and a handkerchief value 4d., at Hertford Quarter Sessions. She was burned in the hand in open court.

Claiming of benefit became increasingly frequent. Of the twenty-five prisoners presented at the Hertford Gaol Delivery of 1st March 1591, 9 were found guilty and sentenced or remanded, 11 were found guilty but claimed benefit and 5 were discharged not guilty. At about the same time at St. Albans, Thomas Pasgrave, John Mychell and Thomas Whaler, alias Whelers, confessed to cattle stealing - a serious offence. They too pleaded benefit, and were released. In 1593, William Long and Richard Corbett were indicted for prison breaking at Hertford. They pleaded benefit, and were discharged. All are typical cases.

But not everyone was successful in their plea. In 1615 Christopher Burkbey of Wiggington was a carpenter, but turned to sheep stealing (21 of them). He claimed benefit of clergy, but was found to be unable to read, and was hanged. At the same Assizes Charles Seawell, of Royston, was found guilty of the theft of three cows. He could not read either, and suffered the same fate.

Offences were divided into those with or without benefit of clergy. Conviction under Henry VIII's Witchcraft Act of 1542 for example was without benefit.

Benefit began to be used as a method of mitigating harsh sentences, and on occasion the judiciary even advised the accused to claim it. It was finally abolished in 1827.

To return to Ecclesiastical Courts: those they condemned were passed to a secular court for sentence, as the church had no powers to harm those it condemned, other than ordering penance or excommunication. They had prisons of their own, but they were used for the holding of persons awaiting trial, not for their punishment. There was no right to bail for those confined by Ecclesiastical Courts.

Apart from civil cases, the most common offences heard were blasphemy, perjury and sexual offences such as fornication and adultery, so much so that they were sometimes called "bawdy courts."

Any criminal jurisdiction that was left was abolished in 1641. There was a brief period under Charles II during which the power to try minor offences was revived, but the power of the church in criminal matters was gone.

Ecclesiastical Courts sit today, but they now concern themselves with church matters alone; most of the offences they used to try are no longer illegal.

The Magna Carta of 1215 had some clauses affecting the administration of justice:

Clauses 18-19:	"...two justices are to be sent through the realm four times a year and with four knights of each county chosen by the county are to hold the Assizes on the day and in the meeting place of the Shire Court. If all cannot be taken on the day, enough knights and freeholders are to remain to conduct the business."
Clause 38:	"No bailiff upon his own bare word without credible witness is to send a man to the ordeal."
Clause 45:	"No justice [is] to be appointed but that he knows the law and is willing to observe it."

Around this time appear mentions of another court - the 'Pie-powder Court.' The name is said to derive from 'pieds poudres' (dusty feet), and the court was constituted in market towns to dealt with minor offences concerning wrongdoers from outside of the area. The name suggests a Norman origin, but it may be older. There were many of them, including Baldock and Chipping Barnet.

Edward I attempted to suppress the worst abuses of the Manor Courts. The frequency of their assembly was set at every four weeks but they rarely seem to have complied with this, some meeting annually or less. Most importantly, however, the detail of the Assize Court system that was to last until 1971 was laid down.

A Grand Jury of between twelve and twenty-three freeholders of the county sat to hear the 'bills' to be presented to the court, containing the evidence for the prosecution. A jury for each hundred was sworn in. It was their job to decide whether there was a case to answer or not; if they thought that there was, they returned a verdict of a "True Bill" (*Billa Vera*). If they were not convinced, the verdict was "not a True Bill," "Not Found" or "*Ignoramus.*" *Ignoramus* literally meant, "we have no knowledge of," and was a relic of the time when the Grand Jury was expected to indict wrongdoers from their own local knowledge, which, in theory, they still did. A Grand Jury verdict that there was no case to answer did not save the accused from future prosecution, as he had not been tried. The principle of double jeopardy did not apply. If further evidence came to light, the case could be re-presented.

Assuming that the verdict was for a True Bill, the accused stood trial at Court of Assize, where cases of all types were heard before the Justices under the organisation of the Clerks of the Assize. Later, the same system was used at the Quarter Sessions, where the Clerk of the Peace was the regulating official.

In the early 19th century, and presumably for many years before, the Assizes were viewed as an entertainment for those fortunate enough not to appear before them. John Carrington recorded in his diary for March 1807:

"Thursday 5 To the Assizes Judge Heath... only Law the First Day..." The day was taken up with civil cases, which Carrington seems to have found uninteresting. Not to be put off, he went back the next day, only to be disappointed again:

"Fryday 6 To the Assizes againe but Such a Crowd could(nt) hare or See So Spent at falkrn (the Falcon Inn) wth Pooll & Clockmaker 9d..."

Almost exactly a year later he had a better day.

"Fryday 4 To Hartford againe to the Assizes, Simmonds the murderer from Hoddesdon I saw Cast and Condemed, as to be hung on Monday next..." Thomas Simmonds, or Simmons, had murdered Sarah Hammerstone of Hoddesdon in the course of attacking Sarah Harris, who had rejected his advances. He was hanged on Monday, 7th March 1808.

The Statute of Gloucester was Edward's attempt to crack down on private courts, such as those held within a liberty. Commissioners were sent out to investigate them, and ask for evidence from the lords holding them of their right to do so. Following strong resistance by the barons, a compromise was reached. Provided there was evidence of their existence at the coronation of Richard I in 1157, the courts were permitted to continue. In many cases no such evidence existed, and the courts were dissolved.

The 14th century saw some reorganisation. The country was divided into circuits, Hertfordshire being assigned to the Home Circuit, and a new court called the Quarter Sessions was created. It dealt with less significant cases than the Assizes, which became the court for only the most serious trials. Edward III had appointed three justices for Hertfordshire in 1327, and in 1336 he appointed seven. Their powers were extended and numbers increased by the Justices of the Peace Act of 1361. As in the Assize Court, the evidence was heard first by the Grand Jury, and if they found a True Bill, the case was tried before a the court and a second jury.

From the middle of the century the Justices usually sat at least four times a year, hence the name Quarter Sessions. From 1388 they were required to do so, though they could meet more often if they so wished. The Sessions were at Epiphany (6 January), Easter, Midsummer (24 June) and Michaelmas (29 September).

There were four Courts of Quarter Sessions in Hertfordshire. In addition to county sessions, held at Hertford and St. Albans, both of these towns held Borough Sessions, dealing with cases arising within their own jurisdictions.

Conviction rates were low: of those accused, only 30-40% came to trial, and of those, only 20-25% were convicted.

From 1461, all indictments heard at the Sheriff's Tourn at the Hundred Courts were transferred to the Quarter Sessions. The old courts hung on as relics for many years to come, in fact until 1867. The County Court Act of that year decreed that no case should be brought before a Hundred Court if it fell within the jurisdiction of the new County Courts. This often causes some confusion. The Shire and Hundred Courts at some stage in their history became known as County Courts, but they were not in any way connected with these new County Courts.

The situation at the end of the 15th century, then, was this: there was a new court structure in place, consisting of Quarter Sessions, Assizes, and the King's Court (the *Curia Regis*). Trial by ordeal was prohibited, except trial by battle, and that was rarely used. The Grand and Petty Juries decided matters of fact, and the justices, either in Assize or Quarter Sessions, dispensed the law. The Assize Court hearings were divided into Gaol Delivery - the trial of prisoners in custody; and Oyer and Terminer, which tried cases deemed to have broken the King's Peace. A number of archaic courts still existed - the Hundred and Manor Courts for example, and they were not to disappear for many years to come; their importance was slight however, and declining all the time.

Despite the powers of the King's Court, the Common Law was being enforced to the letter in the early part of the 16th century, with little consideration for justice. Cardinal Wolsey, as Lord Chancellor, used the court of the Star Chamber to great effect to enforce the principle of equity. Wolsey's view was that it was the *intention* of the law that should be enforced. For example, a law of Edward III of 1341 stated that no alms should be given to a beggar who could work, on pain of imprisonment for the donor. Did this mean that, should you come upon such a person in a snowstorm, poorly clad, you should let him freeze to death? Of course not, said Wolsey; that was not the intention of the legislators, and, in equity, there should be no penalty for aiding the beggar.

Law and Disorder in Hertfordshire

The first mention of the Star Chamber is in 1398, with reference to a 'Sterred Chambre' at the Palace of Westminster. The name seems to refer to ceiling decoration, and it is from this that the Star Chamber got its name. It was a criminal court, presided over by the King's counsel. In its early days it tried those too great to try in the normal courts, but later its jurisdiction was widened.

In the middle of the 16th century, following outbreaks of the plague in London, the Star Chamber sat under Sir Nicholas Bacon at Hertford Castle, along with other courts normally sitting in the capital city.

Cases came from all over the country. In these examples from Hertfordshire in the early 17th century, it is worth noting that, in common with other courts, the cases were brought by individuals, not on their behalf by a prosecutor or the crown.

Plaintiff	Defendant(s)	Offence
William Foster, & Ellen, his wife.	Thos. Weeks, Alexander Allwyn, Peter La Meare, Sarah his wife and others.	False imprisonment arising from a dispute over land in Rickmansworth.
William Stearn of Nuthampstead, gentleman.	Robert Chester of Cockenhatch, Knight, JP.	Assault near defendant's house arising out of a land dispute as to the price of land in Barkway, and binding the plaintiff over to keep the peace without cause.
Daniel Evans of Hadley, plasterer.	Edmund Goohere and others, of St. Albans.	Perjury in support of divers indictments of robbery at St. Albans and Hadley.
John Steadman of Whitecross Street, London, yeoman.	John Brockett, Cressey Bardolf, John Gibson and others.	The rescue of the said Bardolf from arrest for debt at Wheathampstead.

The Star Chamber was finally abolished in 1641 by the Long Parliament, during the Civil War. During its lifetime it had been an extremely popular institution, being referred to by contemporary writers as "a most noble and praiseworthy court," and "one of the sagest and noblest institutions of this kingdom."

The 16th and 17th centuries saw the decline of the Manor Court to little more than a means of recording the transfer of land. There was corresponding growth in the power of the Vestry, which arose from acts of parliament promoting the parish as a convenient centre for local administration. The Vestry had been in existence for many years, as the receiver of church dues; now it became responsible for everything from the appointment of constables to the maintenance of highways. From 1601 it was obligated to erect a poor house, and collect and distribute the poor rate.

By the end then of the 17th century the court structure was firmly established, and changes, with a few exceptions, were administrative. It is with one of these exceptions that we enter the 18th century.

As a result of the heavy workload on the Quarter Sessions, Justices of the Peace in the hundreds began to organise regular sittings called "Petty Sessions." These sittings were in time to become the local Magistrates' Courts, which sat, and still sit, in the larger towns of the county. Jurisdiction was over minor offences only, and the penalties available to the court were limited. Nevertheless, the changes meant that country squires and gentlemen had to learn some law; especially when, in the mid 19th century, Clerks to the Justices were obliged to send details of punishments, and shortly afterwards case papers as well, to the Clerks of the Peace at the subsequent Quarter Sessions.

By the late 18th century it was common for Clerks of Assize and Clerks of the Peace to pay the justices for their posts. Their position could be a lucrative one, as fees were charged at almost every opportunity. The Clerks of Assize for the Home Circuit, which included Hertfordshire, charged the following fees on conviction:

Burnt in the Hand	4s. 8d.
Whipped	4s. 8d.
Acquitted	8s. 4d.
Discharged by Proclamation	8s. 4d.
Recording every Ignoramus of a Felony	6s. 4d.

A few years later the Clerk of the Peace for the Borough of St. Albans Quarter Sessions charged 6s. 8d. for the discharge of a prisoner by proclamation, and 3s. 6d. for "writing a Letter by order of the Magistrates to Major Jones C. O. 6th. Regt. Foot, informing him of Conviction and Sentence of John Wallis, James Warwick & John Warwick." In most instances the clerks of the other circuits charged more.

Two important rights were granted to the accused: in 1836, they were given the right to representation in court, and to know what evidence was to be presented against them. And in 1898 prisoners were for the first time given the right to give evidence on their own behalf.

A further impediment to justice existed that was not to disappear for many years to come. The public taste for gruesome detail had been catered for in the past by privately printed pamphlets. Accuracy was not a prerequisite, and these tracts often catered to the basest of instincts. With the rise of newspapers, inaccurate reporting became a scandal. The accused were judged in the papers long before their trials. Perhaps even worse was the practice of staging plays about the crime before the trial, usually incorporating as props items actually involved in the offence, the bloodier the better. An example was the case of John Thurtell and Joseph Hunt, accused in 1823 of the murder of William Weare. Mr. Justice Parke broke off his summing up to denounce "the prejudice which has been raised against both prisoners through the press." This generated numerous pamphlets, one of which even claimed that Weare was still alive! Hunt was transported and Thurtell was hanged at Hertford. It is said that the executioner was drunk.

A few years after the closure of the prison in Ware Road, Hertford in 1878, a concerted effort was made to get the Assizes moved to St. Albans. Leaflets were circulated by both sides, and a public meeting held. The reasons for the proposed move had some validity. The county Gaol was at St. Albans, and the transport of prisoners some 14 miles to Hertford, and lodging them while they were there, was expensive. There was a risk of escape in transit, and finally the courthouse in Hertford was in poor condition. Nonetheless, the Assizes stayed where they where. There were, after all, 18 cells beneath the Shire Hall at Hertford, whilst St. Albans had much less accommodation for prisoners waiting to be brought before the court.

In the procedures of the courts there was some progress too. Before 1879 prosecution was the responsibility of the victim, unless they were fortunate enough to live in an area where the Clerks of the Peace or the police carried out that function. The Prosecution of Offenders Act appointed the Director of Public Prosecutions, reporting to the Attorney General, to be responsible for criminal prosecution.

The Boroughs of both Hertford and St. Albans had lost their Quarter Sessions under the Municipal Corporations Act of 1835. In Hertford's case it had been abolished, but in St. Albans the Borough and Liberty Sessions were merged. Now, almost forty years later, the Liberty lost its own Commission of the Peace, a privilege that it had had for centuries. Hertfordshire was split into two regions for Quarter Sessions: the Hertford Region, consisting of the area to the east of the western border of Kimpton, Ayot St. Lawrence, Ayot St. Peter, Hatfield and North Mimms; and the Liberty of St. Albans Region (though NOT as a liberty) the rest of the county. The Quarter Sessions were held in the two towns.

There was between 1872 and 1874 a reorganisation and simplification of the courts under Gladstone's Lord Chancellor, Lord Selborn. The Court of Common Pleas was combined with the King's Bench under the name of the King's Bench Division. As part of rationalisation, Hertfordshire was transferred to the South-east Circuit. It had been part of the Home Circuit for Assizes since 1558.

Until 1907 there was no appeal from the Quarter Sessions or the Assizes other than on a question of law. There had been thirty bills put before the House of Commons between 1844 and 1904 on this subject; all had failed. The Criminal Appeal Act finally established the Court of that name. It consisted of the Lord Chief Justice and eight justices of the King's Bench Division, normally with three sitting for each case. The convicted person could appeal on a question of law, a point of fact, or against the sentence (unless convicted of a fixed-sentence offence). In most cases the appeal had to be made within ten days. As a result, no corporal or capital sentence could be carried out until the ten days were up. In important cases, appeal to the House of Lords was provided for.

Inconsistency of sentencing has always been a problem with judicial systems. Until the 20th century, justices often had considerable leeway in the sentences they handed down. This leeway has been eroded considerably over the last 100 years, and continues to be a bone of contention.

The Criminal Justice (Amendment) Act of 1926 allowed the courts to order the accused to pay costs, damages or compensation, as well as the penalties provided in law for their offence.

There were reforms too of the courts. After the Administration of Justice Act of 1933 the Grand Jury was called no more. Later the Quarter Sessions and the Assizes went too, replaced by the Crown Courts in 1971.

Where Courts were Held

There have been too many courthouses in Hertfordshire to mention more than a small sample.

In the medieval period, courts were frequently held out of doors, especially when large numbers of people were involved. The Hundred Court of the Abbot's Liberty of St. Albans was held beneath an ash tree in the Abbey courtyard, and Wymondley Manor Court sat outside in the summer.

Other early courts were held in castles. Courts Baron and Leet were held at Berkhamsted Castle. Other buildings would be pressed into service as and where they were available, inns being popular. Hertford Quarter Sessions were held for a while at an inn, and the Petty Sessions for Welwyn were held at the White Hart for 50 years before 1900. In Baldock the Archdeacon's court was

Law and Disorder in Hertfordshire

held at the George and Dragon in 1591. Coroner's Courts were frequently held in inns, and it was common practice to take dead bodies to the nearest public house, where the inquest was held. A typical example was the inquest on William Weare in 1823, which was held at the Artichoke Inn in Elstree.

Berkhamsted - the Old Court House

Above: the Old Courthouse at Berkhamsted. The main structure is Elizabethan. (author)

Again at Berkhamsted, there still exists the old Court House in Church Lane (once called Back Lane). It is a much-modified Elizabethan building, tucked away behind the High Street, near the parish church. When it was built, it faced directly onto the High Street. The buildings now between the two are later additions. The timbers are original, but the porch, windows and door are not; nor are the brick and flint facing. The 1598 borough charter stated that "ye bayliffe and burgesses should have and hold within ye borough, one court of record, to be holden on Tuesday, once in every month..."

Later the "Courts of the Honour and Manor of Berkhamsted" were held in the building at Whitsuntide and Michaelmas. The constables and other officers were appointed at this sitting, as well as the usual court business being transacted.

The Court of Port-mote, or Borough Court was also held in the building. Since then the building has been used for a number of purposes, including a school.

St. Albans

After the Peasants' Revolt in 1381, John Ball was tried at St. Albans Moot hall. Just where this was situated in now uncertain. A building that had once served as a courthouse was given to the town at the time of the first charter, and it may be that they were in fact the same building. The latter structure was in the Market Place, and was to become the Town House or Town Hall. The Compter prison was beneath the room used by the Borough court; the same area was also used to store the mobile stocks and pillory. The County Court (the Hundred and Shire Courts) justices usually sat in a room in the Abbey Gatehouse.

Above: the old Town Hall and courthouse at St. Albans. The Borough Gaol, or Compter, was in the same building. Based on an illustration from around 1797. (author).

The old Town Hall was in poor condition by the early 19th century, and all agreed that it needed to be replaced. The argument over what to replace it with, and where, lasted for some time.

Finally the current site of the Town Hall was agreed upon. The next question was, where was the money to come from? Eventually a compromise was reached whereby a two-thirds share was to be paid by the county, and one third by the borough. The building work started in 1829, and was completed in 1831. The courtroom was an integral part of the structure, and was used from 1831-1966, when a new building was constructed. There were two cells beneath the court to house those due to appear in the dock, one for males and one for females.

Above: the new Town Hall in St. Albans. The court was held on the first floor. (Museum of St. Albans). Below: the Shire Hall at Hertford, built in 1769/70. (Hertford Museum)

HERTFORD.
(The Town Hall &c.)

Hertford

In 1769-70, a new Shire Hall was built on the site of the old Elizabethan Town Hall, which was in a dilapidated condition, and too small for the business with which it had to deal. The design was by James Adams, one of the celebrated brothers responsible for so much civic work in England. A different site had been considered, but the plans fell through, and the original site was used following demolition of the old building. The cost was more than £7,500, more than £2,500 above the estimate, and was met by an addition to the county rates. A fine clock by John Briant was added in 1824.

The new building was designed to house both criminal and civil courts, as well as a corn exchange. There were two courtrooms, the original intention being that one would deal with criminal cases, the other civil.

Hitchin Magistrates' and Juvenile Courts

Above left: the Sun Hotel in Hitchin, where for many years the magistrates sat. Above right: Hitchin Police Station and Magistrates' Court. The magistrates sat on the first floor. Further accommodation was built to the rear of the station in 1937. (author)

The Hitchin magistrates used to meet at the Sun Inn. Next door, at the Angel Inn, now demolished, sat an ecclesiastical court, that of the Archdeacon of Huntingdon.

Law and Disorder in Hertfordshire

In December 1879 instructions were issued to look for a site for a new Police Station and Courtroom for the Petty Sessions. There were practical advantages in combining the two - prisoners could be brought directly from the cells to the court.

There were three cells, seven feet by thirteen feet, and a prisoners' yard. The courtroom was to be forty-four feet by twenty-two feet, with withdrawing rooms in addition.

The complex was built with an arch leading into the yard. The cells were to the right of the yard, behind the enquiry desk and parade room. The new premises were completed in 1885.

By 1937 the courthouse was no longer large enough, and additional accommodation was built behind the Police Station. Work was completed in 1939.

Both buildings still stand, but neither are used for their original purpose, having been vacated in 1973. The Police Station is now a youth centre.

Chapter Three

Punishment

The reasons for punishing offenders consist of some or all of the following elements:

> deterrence - to stop others from committing the same offence.
> retribution - vengeance against the offender.
> incapacitation - to remove the offender from circulation, and thus reduce repeat crimes.
> rehabilitation - to reintroduce the offender into society after reforming his criminal behaviour.

Arguments have raged for centuries over what does and does not work. The matter can be a highly emotive one. A high profile crime can, and has, resulted in changes to the law out of all proportion to the offence committed.

Down the centuries, society has used numerous methods for dealing with offenders, some surprisingly enlightened for their time, but for the most part brutal.

Imprisonment

Prisoners have been confined in oubliettes, local lock-ups or cages, houses of correction, ecclesiastical gaols, county gaols and convict prisons. Hertfordshire has never had a convict prison, and I have been unable to trace any oubliettes, but we have had examples of all the rest.

Imprisonment was not originally intended as a punishment, but as a method of restraint of those yet to come to trial. Incarceration methods in England, like so much of our justice system, have grown rather than been planned.

The dividing line between a gaol and a prison is a fine one. Both words are defined in the dictionary in the same way; both have almost identical pedigrees from at least the 13th century. And should it be a gaol or a jail? Both spellings are acceptable and in current usage. The choice then depends as much as anything upon the whim of the writer, and carries no significance.

Early Confinement

Early gaols were not regulated in any way. Many were privately owned, perhaps by a local baron or a senior member of the church. Conditions varied enormously. Some (though precious few) were quite humane. The majority reflected their age - they were brutal, cold, damp places from which inmates were often lucky to emerge alive.

Law and Disorder in Hertfordshire

In 1166 the Assize of Clarendon directed the building of gaols in all counties and boroughs under local authority, but there was still no regulation of them. The law had no interest in the method of confinement; that was the gaoler's business. He was responsible for restraining the prisoner, and delivering him or her for trial or punishment. How he did it was up to him.

A gaol was no more than a building in which prisoners were confined. Ideas of mighty fortresses with high walls and barred windows must be discarded. Security might indeed be by the nature of the structure - solid walls, strong doors, barred windows, good locks and so on. But it was just as likely to be achieved with chains and fetters, in a building that looked much the same as those around it. The latter was often preferred as the cheaper option. Rarely was the gaol purpose-built. In some cases prisoners were confined in public houses, and concern was sometimes expressed when they appeared before the justices drunk and unfit to plead.

The Sheriff of the County was made responsible for the County Gaol in medieval times, and remained so until 1531 when responsibility was transferred to the Quarter Sessions. This did not mean that other gaols did not exist; the Liberty of St. Albans had its own gaol, as did the Borough of Hertford. Ecclesiastical Courts, whilst they had no power actually to harm those that appeared before them, could incarcerate them pending trial. It should not be thought that courts under the control of the church or churchmen were better than the rest. At the gaol at Ely - the direct responsibility of the Bishop - the structure was so dilapidated that the gaoler felt it necessary to chain the prisoners on their backs to prevent escape.

The gaol population in England was made up of three groups: those awaiting trial; those tried and sentenced to a period of detention; and debtors. Until 1869, a person in debt could be imprisoned, and they frequently were. In some gaols, debtors outnumbered criminals.

By 1729 reported abuses in the gaols of England had reached serious proportions. There were a number of convictions for cruel treatment and even the murder of prisoners, and an act was passed that was intended to curb the worst excesses. It was widely ignored by local justices, and the abuse continued for another fifty years.

The post of gaoler was usually sold to the highest bidder. He recouped his outlay by charging fees from the prisoners. He received no salary - he made his living, and a comfortable living it could be, from what he could extract from the men and women in his charge. They had to pay to be committed the gaol, to appear in court, they were even charged if they were freed by the court as innocent. They paid too for their food and lodging. The more they could pay, the better was their accommodation. If they could not pay, they stayed in gaol. The gaoler also controlled the food supply, bedding and other necessities that came into the gaol, and the prices of them. He had a monopoly on everything the prisoners had to have to survive.

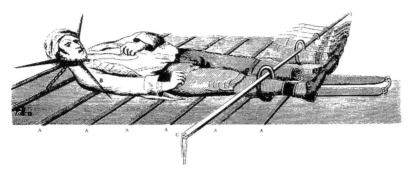

Above: prisoners at Ely gaol. A complaint was made to the Crown by the Grand Jury in 1764 that the gaoler restrained the prisoners with irons. The Privy Council took proceedings against the bishop for not maintaining the gaol. (from William Hepworth Dixon's "John Howard and the Prison World of Europe")

Alcohol was on sale in gaols, and in many of them new prisoners were charged a fee called "garnish," which was used to procure liquor for the existing inmates. Failure to pay resulted in running the gauntlet. In Hertford Gaol in 1729 the garnish was set at 4s. 6d.

In theory, prisoners convicted of a felony were entitled to the county allowance, or county bread as it was commonly known. This was a small allowance, given in money or food, to keep body and soul together. The problem was that where the allowance was given in money, inflation reduced its value. In some counties it was as low as 1d. per day; in others as much as 2d. In Hertfordshire in 1672, Phillip Trindall petitioned the justices at Hertford, claiming that as a poor prisoner, he could not afford the 4d. daily lodging fee charged by the gaoler, and asked to be allowed the "1d. provided for in the act." Towards the end of the 18th century there was a move towards giving a fixed quantity of food per day. In Hertford this was set at a daily allowance of 16 ounces of bread, later increased to 24 ounces.

There was no allowance made for debtors, nor, according to the Privy Council, did "prisoners being in prison on suspicion of having committed an offence, have any right to support and maintenance from the Sheriff or gaoler." In many cases however the allowances for felons were extended to other classes of prisoner as well. The prisoners' rations could be supplemented by friends or family from the outside. Indeed, most of the unpleasant aspects of being in gaol could be alleviated if one had money.

Law and Disorder in Hertfordshire

In 1773, John Howard of Bedford was appointed Sheriff of his county. Unlike most other sheriffs of his time, he took the post seriously, and looked into the conditions at the county gaol. He was appalled by what he found, particularly regarding fees, and recommended to the justices that the gaoler be paid a salary instead. He was asked to find out what was done in other counties, and to his dismay he found that the practice of charging fees seemed widespread. He therefore undertook a survey of prisons throughout Britain. His findings were published as *The State of the Prisons*, and resulted in the Prisons Act of 1778. This book provides us with a snapshot of most of the gaols of the time. Where they still exist the reports to the Quarter Sessions can also be illuminating, always provided that the investigators carried out their duty.

Despite the act, abuses continued, and the new regulations were frequently ignored. The justices responsible for inspecting the gaols frequently neglected their inspections through idleness or fear of contracting typhus, also known as gaol fever.

The disease is due to a micro-organism spread by human body or head lice, and therefore occurs where people are crammed together. For that reason it was also known as ship, camp or war fever. It is of small consolation that the micro-organism eventually kills the louse. Unscrupulous gaolers played upon fear to try to keep out those justices that insisted on making the inspections that the 1778 act required. The fear was not an irrational one; many prisoners, and some gaolers, died of typhus.

The insanitary state of the gaols also allowed typhoid and cholera to spread, through faecal-oral contact, usually through wells infected by nearby privies, or unhygienic food preparation. Even flies could spread these diseases. (Typhoid and typhus were frequently confused, hence the similarity in the name).

Howard said he avoided disease by trusting in divine providence, and rarely drawing a deep breath in an offensive room. That he survived for as long as he did was therefore pure luck.

Cages

Most small communities had a lock-up, or cage. Its purpose was to contain prisoners for short periods only, until they could be released (perhaps after sobering up) or brought before a justice before being transferred to more central accommodation. There were many designs, from sturdy wooden sheds to quite ornate structures. There may have been a bench or seat inside, but no other 'comforts.' Even as an overnight lodging they must have been unpleasant, especially as no sanitation more sophisticated than a bucket would have been available. They remained in use until supplanted by their logical successor - the police cell. Where no cage existed, other buildings might be used - the Royal Oak in Hemel Hempstead was pressed into service to detain offenders on occasion.

Houses of Correction or Bridewells

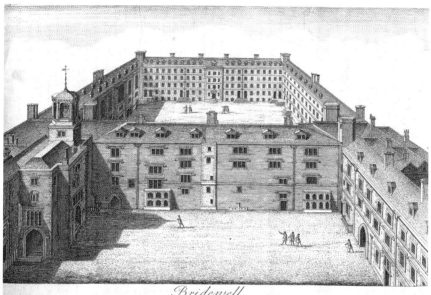

Above: the original Bridewell Gaol in London. Note the stocks in the nearer of the two courtyards. (from a contemporary print)

Houses of correction were set up as the result of an act of 1609, but had their origins in the workhouses under the Elizabethan Poor Law Acts in 1576. They became known as bridewells after Bridewell Gaol in London, upon which they were modelled, and the two terms were used interchangeably. The original Bridewell was in the district between Fleet Street and the Thames, on the banks of the Fleet river, and was named after the well of St. Bride or St Bridget which was located nearby. The building had been put up by Henry VIII, and in 1553 it was given over by Edward VI as a penitentiary for 'vagbonds and loose women.' Beneath a portrait of Edward was a notice board:

> *This Edward of fair memory the Sixt,*
> *In whom with greatness, goodness was comixt,*
> *Gave this Bridewell, a palace in olden times,*
> *For a chastening house of vagrant crimes.*

Most of the original buildings were lost in the Great Fire of 1666, but the institution did not close until 1855.

The purpose of the new bridewells was the confinement of dissolute paupers and idle apprentices; places of compulsory employment for vagrants and others out of work (an act of 1667 empowered the justices to levy a rate of up to 6d. per parish to provide raw materials to keep the inmates working). For a hundred years they provided a useful if harsh service to the community, but by the end of the seventeenth century they had become small local prisons. This change of use was recognised by act of Parliament in 1720, when the justices were authorised to commit vagrants and minor offenders to the gaol or the bridewell as they saw fit. In fact, the bridewells came to be used for holding petty offenders, vagrants, and those awaiting trial. Concern was expressed that if prisoners on remand were sent to the County Gaols they would emerge as fully trained criminals.

An interesting submission to the county justices exists concerning the possible closure of the bridewell at Hitchin in 1789, which echoes a concern expressed down the centuries:

> "The inhabitants of Hitchin in Vestry assembled beg leave with the utmost respect to represent to His Majesty's Justices of the Peace for this County the inconvenience which they are apprehensive would follow from the removal of the Bridewell from Hitchin. They conceive that the Hundreds of Hitchin and Broadwater which include the towns of Hitchin and Baldock and are situate at one of the extremities of the County, are of such an extent as to require a prison of this nature.
> "That the conveyance of persons convicted of small offences and for short periods, so far as Hertford will be attended with a heavy expense, and is so much trouble as to prevent or at very least very much check such prosecutions.
> "That this Bridewell is of great use for the confinement of persons committed for further examination and if it should be suppressed great inconvenience is to be expected from the keeping of such persons in Public Houses, which not only occasions a heavy charge upon the Prosecutor or the Parish but improper persons very often get access to the prisoner so confined and in many instances the prisoner is suffered to drink too freely and is brought before the Magistrate in an improper state.
> "They have confidence that if one general Bridewell should be established for the County the wisest regulations will be framed, but they fear from what has occurred in every other large prison, even those that are best managed, young and petty offenders will by being associated with more atrocious criminals come from such a place hardened and made worse instead of that amendment which may be hoped for in a place of solitary confinement.
> "They are aware that some alterations are necessary in the present Bridewell; they are perfectly willing to pay the utmost attention to any

direction of the Magistrates for rendering this more fit for the purposes it is intended.

"They humbly request therefore that the Justices will be pleased to continue the present Bridewell and to give such order for its improvement as they shall in their wisdom think necessary."

The bridewell stayed open.

The Growth of the Victorian Prison System
In order to understand what happened in Hertfordshire's county gaols, it is necessary to look first at the nation's prison system, culminating in the Victorian monolith that it became.

Howard's work had revitalised measures that had failed to clear parliament. Immediately following his evidence to the House of Commons in 1774 two acts were passed: "An Act for preserving the health of prisoners in gaol and preventing the gaol distemper," (typhus), and "An Act for the relief of prisoners who shall be acquitted or discharged." The provisions of the acts were to be displayed in all houses of detention, as was the scale of gaolers' fees.

The first act provided for regular cleansing of gaols, and their inmates, and the provision of sick rooms and doctors. The second act addressed the problem of those that could not afford the fees for release. In future, charging prisoners a fee for release was prohibited, and the gaoler's fees were to be met from the county rate.

Based upon Howard's principles, though not drafted by him, the Penitentiary Act of 1779 started a controversy that was to last more than a hundred years.

The act provided for the building of national penitentiaries to take the prisoners that had been sentenced to transportation. As a result of the American War of Independence, from 1776 they could no longer be sent to the Americas, and an alternative was yet to be found. The penitentiaries were to be secure and sanitary, open to systematic inspection, without fees, and be run under a reformatory regime.

Previously, a sentence of imprisonment had been intended to address three of the four reasons for punishment: deterrence, retribution and incapacitation. Reformation, or rehabilitation, would follow through fear of repeat punishment. Actually to address reformation of offenders was unusual. Unfortunately the principle was lost, as none of the proposed prisons were built, and transportation resumed in 1784, to a new destination: Australia.

Some principles did not disappear however. Communication between prisoners was forbidden. When not working, the prisoners were to be locked in their cells. Whenever contact was unavoidable, they were to be subject to continuous supervision. It was this matter of communication that caused the controversy, as will shortly be seen.

Labour of the most servile kind was required of the prisoner, though where possible this should be profitable. Attendance of religious service was compulsory, though only Anglicans, Catholics and Jews were provided for.

Despite, or because of, the abandonment of the national penitentiaries, some counties petitioned for acts to be passed permitting them to build new gaols (Hertfordshire included), and the principles of the 1779 act appeared in some of this later legislation.

In 1791 the Prisons Act was passed. Like much legislation of the time, this act was permissive: it allowed the Quarter Sessions to reform prisons, but it did not compel them to do so. The act was muddled and poorly drafted, and left the situation much as it had been before Howard started his campaign. And now the Napoleonic Wars ensured that other matters employed the minds of government. In 1812 the Prison Discipline Society, which had continued Howard's work, reported that the gaols were "relapsing into their former horrid state of privation, filthiness, cruelty and neglect".

Thus there had been little progress for 25 years, though there were agitators for reform. In 1815, an Act was passed making the claiming of fees a criminal offence, though little was done to enforce it. The next few years saw some activity, notably Sir Robert Peel's consolidating act of 1823, clarifying the responsibility of the Quarter Sessions for the county gaols and bridewells. Sidney Smith and others blamed the rise in the prison population in the 1820's on what they saw as the pleasant conditions in the gaols, and it is in this period that the principle of "less eligibility" arises, though not under that name. A person in prison, they said, should not expect to live better than a free labourer outside. The problem was that there was no agreement as to what a "free labourer" was, or could be expected to earn. The same principle was applied to the workhouses. Deterrence became the goal, and a severe prison regime advocated. Prisoners should suffer, in order that they should be too frightened to re-offend.

Prisoners on remand received the same treatment as those adjudged guilty in court, even though they were, in theory, innocent until proven guilty. About one third of those charged could expect to be acquitted, so a large number of people were punished without justification.

Arguments raged back and forth over a number of aspects of prison discipline, but it was all a waste of time, because until 1835 there was no independent supervision of the gaols. In that year a select committee from the House of Lords recommended the appointment of government inspectors, though responsibility for the gaols was unchanged. They also recommended the "silent" rather than the "separate" system of prison discipline. These two terms require some explanation.

The "silent" system meant that when working or exercising prisoners were supervised, and not permitted to speak to one another. When not working or exercising, they were locked in their cells. This was the system recommended by John Howard.

The "separate" system kept the prisoner in his cell, where he worked, ate, and slept. His only communication was with the prison officers and the occasional visit by the governor or chaplain. Both regimes were intended to encourage the prisoner to contemplate his situation and the folly of his crime.

The Prisons Act of 1835 implemented the Committee's recommendations, including the silent system.

The separate system was not to be killed off so easily. In 1850 the Select Committee on Prison Discipline, known as the Grey Committee, found that the application of prison regulations was patchy, and there was a good deal of variation in conditions across the country. They recommended consistency of treatment of offenders, and the introduction of the separate system. The majority of the recommendations were implemented.

The effect of the isolation on prisoners under the separate system varied. Some spent as much of their time as possible asleep. Others paced. Prisoners had conversations with themselves. The suicide rate increased. Other than note the rise, the authorities did nothing.

Prisoners' diets were investigated in 1843 and 1864, and recommendations made that were calculated to provide the minimum nourishment necessary to support health. No allowance was made for the size of prisoners, the size of their appetites, or any other variables.

In 1843, for a prisoner serving more than four months, the weekly allowance was

	without hard labour	**with hard labour**
bread	168 ounces	154 ounces
potatoes	32 ounces	112 ounces
meat	12 ounces	16 ounces
total solid food	**212 ounces**	**282 ounces**
soup	3 pints	3 pints
gruel	14 pints	11 pints
cocoa	-	3 pints
total liquid food	**17 pints**	**17 pints**

Those on shorter sentences got less - the minimum, for a man doing less than seven days without hard labour, was 112 ounces of bread and 14 pints of gruel for the week.

The 1864 report concluded that this diet was adequate in most cases; there was rather too little food at the bottom end, but at the other extreme, the cocoa was an unnecessary luxury. Unsurprisingly, they also found that application across the country was irregular.

Around the middle of the century, the colonies refused to accept further convict transportees, (the term "convict" was used exclusively to mean an offender who was transported, or committed to penal servitude in a convict prison). Transportation continued for another fifteen years, but an alternative had to be found. Several government prisons had been built in the first half of the century, and these were to be used to contain prisoners sentenced to penal servitude, designed specifically to house serious offenders. Convicts served a period of solitary confinement, after which they served their time in special public works prisons, where they were employed in land reclamation and the construction of such undertakings as dockyards. As a convict advanced through the progressive stages of confinement, he could earn or lose remission of up to a quarter of his sentence. He was then given a "ticket of leave." Conditions could apply to his release, which, if broken, would result in recommittal.

Above: the treadwheel. Some devices had partitions between the convicts. This one was at Brixton. From a contemporary engraving.

The Carnarvon Committee of 1863 criticised the local gaols for their failure to conform to legislation. Conditions in prisons, they found, still varied enormously. The committee recommended a punitive regime rather than expending effort on rehabilitation.

The committee recommended specific types of hard labour. There were a number of tasks in use across the country, of which the most common were the shot drill, the treadwheel, the crank and oakum picking.

Shot drill consisted of lifting a cannon ball, carrying it a prescribed distance, setting it down and returning to the starting-point. The prisoners were arranged in such a manner that by this time another ball had been delivered by another convict, and the cycle started again. The ball weighed either 24 or 32 pounds, and the drill went on for 75 minutes.

In Ipswich in 1817 William Cubitt devised the treadwheel as a means of ensuring that prisoners worked, and harnessing their labour for some purpose. It consisted of a horizontally mounted wheel, something like a water wheel. The prisoner stepped from one tread to the next as it fell away beneath him, as though he was walking up the outside of the device. He was, of course, going nowhere. Each man was separated from the next by a partition, which created an airless trap. The combination of hard physical exercise and rough prison clothing resulted in the treadwheel being nicknamed 'the cockchafer.' Some reports suggested that prisoners looked forward to their spell on the treadwheel. This was quite untrue - they dreaded it. Fifteen minutes was enough to exhaust all but the fittest of men. Some wheels were used to drive water pumps, ventilators, corn mills and so on, whilst others served no purpose at all. A target was set for the prisoners, but the variation was enormous - the equivalent of climbing anything between 6,000 and 19,400 feet.

The crank was invented by a man called Gibbs. A handle was attached to a horizontal shaft, which entered a drum. On the shaft inside the drum was a series of scoops, similar to a dredger. In the bottom of the drum was either sand or gravel, which was scooped up and deposited by turning the handle. On advanced models there was a revolution counter, and the resistance could be set at different levels. The mechanism could even be mounted outside the prisoner's cell, so that the separate system could be maintained. 10,000 revolutions per day were not uncommon.

In some prisons cranks were organised so that prisoners were actually working against one another, emphasising the pointlessness of the labour.

Oakum picking involved separating the fibres of tarred rope, normally three pounds per day. It was a difficult task unless the prisoner knew what he was doing. A nail was an invaluable aid; without it the target was next to impossible to meet. The finished product might be used to caulk the hulls of wooden boats, or recycled to make rope. Oakum picking was not abandoned until 1929.

The Prisons Act of 1865 implemented the recommendations of the Carnarvon Committee, including uniformity and the separate system. Either the treadwheel or crank was made obligatory for the first part of long sentences.

The result was the closure of many small gaols that could not easily be adapted to meet the new regulations, and the building of some new ones conforming to the new standards.

Above: the crank in use. This illustration is taken from Henry Mayhew, who in the mid 19th century wrote several books highlighting the appalling conditions in London. Of interest is the spartan layout of the cell, and the prison rules displayed on the wall to the right.

The next big step came in 1877. All prisons were taken under government control, and the era of enforced conformity began. Every cell was to be the same size; every prisoner was to receive the same clothing and diet. Their labour was to be identical. Under the first Commissioner of Prisons, Sir Edmund duCane, there was a "fetish of uniformity," and a harsh uniformity at that - "hard work, hard fare and hard bed." The objective was to ensure that every prisoner was treated identically.

Punishment was graduated, and might consist of a reduction in diet, an increase in work, or corporal punishment (whipping was not abolished in England's prisons until 1967). Regulations were draconian; for example the offence of "blowing one's nose in an improper place" invited retribution. A full set of rules hung in each cell, and for the most part they consisted of "thou shalt not..."

A Change of Direction

DuCane retired in 1895, coincidentally in the same year as the Gladstone report. There had been growing criticism of the judicial and penal systems for some time, as it became clear that the twin principles of deterrence and retribution were not working to reduce crime levels. In fact they never had.

Sir Evelyn Ruggles-Brise, duCane's successor, held entirely different views on how prisons and prisoners should be managed. "Reform" now applied to the prisoner, not to the system. The objective was to change the offender's behaviour. Punishment was to become the last resort rather than the first.

Until 1877 it had been easy to blame the failure of the county prisons on local management. In 1895 this was no longer possible - the government had been running the prisons for eighteen years, and the prison population was still rising.

Thought was given to what sort of people went to prison, and for what offences. Why was the level of illiteracy amongst prisoners so high? Why were the same people going to prison time and time again? And why was it that the largest part of the prison population was drawn from the poorest strata of society? The early Victorian belief that each prisoner was fully responsible for what they did - that they chose a life of crime - might be wrong. How, for example, could the poor control the impact that the depression of the late 19th century had upon them? Perhaps a more sympathetic attitude was appropriate.

In 1898 the majority of the prison population was still convicted of petty crime. The average sentence was only twenty-eight days; and more than half of those convicted at the Quarter Sessions had previous convictions.

Measures were passed over the next twenty years that, at least in part, modernised the penal system. The Prisons Act of 1898 contained provisions against excessive corporal punishment, and the abolition of hard labour such as cranks and treadwheels, both of which served no other purpose than to make prisoners suffer and to degrade them. The act also permitted prisoners to earn remission of up to one sixth of their sentence.

Borstals were established for young offenders; parole was made available, depending upon behaviour. A custodial sentence became the last resort of the courts rather than the first. The Children's Act of 1907 reduced imprisonment for children, and established juvenile courts; and the Probation Act of the same year extended the powers of courts to release offenders on their own recognizance. In 1925 it became obligatory for all courts to have a probation officer.

The Criminal Justice Act of 1914 allowed for offenders to be given time to pay fines, rather than committing them to prison straight away.

These measures had dramatic effects. At the start of the 20th century, the average sentence was about 28 days. Less than 1% of inmates were serving a sentence of a year or more, and only 33% more than two weeks. Nearly

Law and Disorder in Hertfordshire

100,000 offenders were sentenced to 14 days or less. By 1926 the figure was under 7,000. At the turn of the century, 600 per 100,000 of the population were imprisoned in any one year. By 1926, that figure had fallen to 115 (the lowest point was in 1918, with 70, presumably due to so many young men being either dead, wounded or serving in the forces).

Ruggles-Brise declared in 1921 that "formerly, prison reform meant the structural reform of the prisons, sanitation, order, cleanliness. Today, it means the reform of the prisoner, by improved methods of influence and treatment while in prison."

By this time, imprisonment in Hertfordshire had ended. The county gaols and bridewells had closed. Cells in police stations had made the cages redundant. Anyone convicted in the future would be held in prisons in other counties. Prisons had become national rather than county institutions.

Hertfordshire Cages

Above: Anstey cage, part of the lychgate. (author)

A survey of lock-ups in Hertfordshire was carried out in 1879, but it does not differentiate between different types - some are clearly cages, others are probably in police stations or court buildings. Nonetheless, some interesting information can be gleaned. Most consisted of one, two or three cells; 22 had a resident keeper (15 did not - in one case he lived 1½ miles away). Only 3 had artificial lighting. Many cells are described as damp and cold. None met government regulations, Watford being closest; but its exercise yard let it down, as it was insecure. Essendon came out worst: it was insecure, small, with insufficient daylight, no ventilation, no heating, and no means of communication with the keeper. There was no closet, and no feeding trap in the door; it was damp and cold, and in a poor state of repair, with no exercise facilities; and the keeper lived ½ mile away. Aldbury, Hoddesdon and Redbourne were nearly as bad. St. Albans cage was located near St. Peter's church, and was erected at a cost of £6 13s. 11d in 1811. The following year it required underpinning. In 1817 there was a formal complaint lodged by the jury of the Court Leet that it was "a great nuisance and very obnoxious to the inhabitants of the neighbourhood." It was eventually removed.

Little is recorded of the inmates of these cages. Shenley once held the murderer of a police constable, and the last inmate is reputed either to have been the landlord of the public house next door, or a deserter from the forces.
There is an enduring story concerning a drunken inmate of these small lock-ups. His friends provide him with further ale, which he consumes through a rush or straw inserted through a knot-hole or a grill in the cage door. In one version the beer is poured through the knot-hole using a kettle. I have found versions of this story in Barton-le-Clay in Bedfordshire, Ashwell and Buntingford. The similarities in the tales are such as to throw some doubt on the story's truth, however charming an anecdote it makes.

At least five cages can still be seen in Hertfordshire:

Anstey	The cage was formed in about 1830 by converting part of the 15th century lychgate to the parish church. It is now used as a shed for gardening tools. It is probably the most picturesque of them all.
Ashwell	Built of blocks of clunch, supposedly from the chantry chapel of Ashwell Church. Clunch is a soft local stone. The chapel was demolished in about 1750, and the cage was built some fifty years later. The roof is slate. It is in a lane called Hodwell, off the High Street, between the church and the springs.
Barley	Situated near the Fox and Hounds public house, the only surviving wooden cage in Hertfordshire, though it is hard to tell whether all the timbers are original. It is thought to date from the late 17th century.
Buntingford	This cage is to be found in Church Street, not far from the Old Croft in Wyddial Road, which used to be Buntingford Bridewell. It is 18th century, built of brick. The top section of the walls was replaced in the 19th century. The building was restored again in the 20th century.

Shenley   The most flamboyant of the cages still existing in Hertfordshire, and right next door to the village pond. It is 18th century, and domed, with a finial. The walls are rendered brick, and very thick. There is a double door, and two windows, above which are the maxims "do well - fear not", and "be sober, be vigilant." There was some restoration work done in 1810, 1893, and again in the 20th century.

Above: the cages at Shenley, left, and Barley, right. (author)

Stevenage cage was dismantled and stored by Stevenage Museum. It is hoped to display at least part of it in the not too distant future.

Many others have disappeared, being built of wood, like that at Cheshunt. It was built in 1721, and cost £9 1s. 2d. to erect. The builder's bill still exists. The cage itself has long since rotted away.

All of the surviving cages in Hertfordshire have a single cell. There is an interesting wooden cage, with two cells, in Roydon, just over the border in Essex.

The cage at Buntingford, above, and Ashwell, below. (author)

Above, the two-cell cage at Roydon. (author)

Hertfordshire Bridewells

Session Rolls for the year of 1598 provide a list of houses of correction in Hertfordshire at that time, with the hundreds they served:

House of Correction	Hundred
Buntingford	Edwinstree
Hatfield	Broadwater
(Hemel) Hempstead	Dacorum
Hitchin	Hitchin
Hoddesdon	Hertford
Royston	Odsey
St. Albans	Cashio
Ware	Braughing

At least two other houses of correction were built later: Berkhamsted in 1674, and Hertford, the first mention of which is 1694.

By 1656 Hatfield, Ware and Hertford seem to have been combined. William Man was master of a single bridewell serving the hundreds of Braughing, Broadwater and Hertford, and was petitioning for funds as the "said house is in great decay."

Above: Buntingford Bridewell, now the Old Croft, in Wyddial Road. (author)

By Howard's time, only five were left: Hertford, The Liberty of St. Albans, Berkhamsted, Buntingford and Hitchin. Over the next hundred years, these went too. Berkhamsted and Hitchin were converted into police stations. The Buntingford bridewell was sold to a private buyer in 1843, and still exists as the Old Croft, in Wyddial Road. The Hemel Hempstead bridewell building also still stands, in the High Street.

The St. Albans bridewell was located in the western part of the Abbey Gatehouse. It served both the Liberty and the Borough of St. Albans. The building is now used for other purposes. Hertford bridewell was been demolished, presumably at the same time as the Ware Road Gaol.

Unlike the county gaols, the keepers of the bridewells seem to have been paid a salary from quite an early date. The number of prisoners was of course much smaller, and sometimes they were empty. Charging of fees was not a practical option, as the keeper would be unpaid during the quiet spells.

There were a number of breaches in security. On 6 March 1760 Oswell Odell "broke and escaped from the House of Correction at Hitchin." At large for three years, he was recaptured, and fined 1s; On 15 March 1785 Eli Kemp and John Huson escaped from Berkhamsted, and did £3 11s. 4d. worth of damage, which had to be made good quickly, as there were other prisoners being held there. Hertford also had a number of escapes.

Law and Disorder in Hertfordshire

John Howard visited Hertfordshire on several occasions. From his reports, perhaps the best of the bridewells was St. Albans, but even that had its drawbacks:

> "The bridewell for the Liberty, and for the Borough, joins to the Liberty Gaol. One large workroom, and two lodging-rooms; all upstairs and airy. No court; no water; no allowance; no straw. Prisoners have their earnings. Clauses against spirituous liquors not hung up. Keeper's salary for the Liberty, £28; for the Borough, £2; no fees. In 1779, I found a girl, who was sentenced for a year's imprisonment, locked up all the day with two soldiers in the workroom; and at my last visit, a girl and a boy were confined together."

1776. 1 March	prisoners	2
1776. 2 Nov.	prisoners	0
1779. 24 April	prisoners	3
1782. 7 May	prisoners	2

The worst were Hitchin and Berkhamsted. John Howard's inspection in Hitchin in 1776 revealed "a room for men $20^{1}/_{2}$ feet by $10^{1}/_{2}$ feet; over it two rooms for women who went up by a ladder. There is no chimney in any room, no straw, no court, no allowance, and no employment." The prisoners of both sexes were described as "quite naked and lousy."

In 1789 magistrates in Quarter Sessions deputed the Rev. Antony Hamilton, D.D., the Rev. Henry Baker, Charles de Laet, William Baker and Adolphus Meetkerke to make an official inspection and report. It adds to the detail given by *The State of the Prisons*:

> "...the building is brick, lined with wood. It has two small windows with shutters which are necessarily shut close every night to prevent people in the yard giving the prisoners implements whereby to escape, which has frequently been done. The upper part is the women's prison divided into two rooms into the roof. The women go up this prison by a ladder on the outside. The Necessary (the latrine) belonging to a very large workhouse adjoins the prison and is excessively offensive. There is no chimney, no water, no opportunity to give any air, no furniture of any kind or any employment... Eight prisoners have been confined at one time in this room. The keeper whose salary is £24 a year maintains prisoners on an allowance of a pound of bread a day and water. He lives more than a quarter of a mile from the prison and only visits it once a day to let out the prisoners for necessary occasions... The keeper declares that the stench from the Necessaries adjoyning the prison is so unwholesome that if prisoners were

detained a fortnight they constantly sickened and generally dyed very soon."

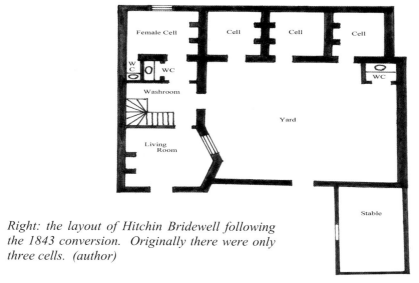

Right: the layout of Hitchin Bridewell following the 1843 conversion. Originally there were only three cells. (author)

In 1807 a new bridewell was built in Hitchin, in Silver Street (now Bancroft). In 1843 it was converted to the town's first police station. It was eventually demolished in 1997 to make way for the entrance to a supermarket.

Howard also reported on the house of correction at Berkhamsted:

"A ward for men, and another for women. A dungeon down nine steps, thirteen feet by nine and a half, and six feet three inches high; each floor very damp, no window; no chimney; no bedsteads; no straw. Keeper's salary, £20; no fees; has the profit of the prisoners' work. They are sometimes employed chopping rags. Allowance a pound of bread a day."

The population of the bridewell was low:

1776. 2 November	prisoners	0
1779. 23 April	prisoners	1
1782. 31 October	prisoners	0

In 1789 the Quarter Sessions ordered that "the Present Dungeon should by no means Employed for the Purpose on Confinm[t]. Either by Day or Night."

By 1826 things had improved. A return on the state of the bridewell at Berkhamsted announces that prisoners were indeed no longer held in the dungeon, which was described as "9 feet irregular and underground." Two upstairs rooms were used instead, one for men, one for women. But there was no fireplace, and the one window was unglazed. The two blankets provided can scarcely have been adequate in the winter. There was a yard, but the keeper considered it so insecure that prisoners were not allowed to use it for exercise. Unfortunately it also housed the only privy, shared by the keeper, his family and the prisoners, and "the keeper or his wife are obliged to attend when any prisoner has occasion to go into the yard." There is no ventilation of the bridewell nor the yard, and "the air is so impure that if prisoners were confined here for any length of time it would produce disease."

Howard does not seem to have visited Hemel Hempstead, but there is a report to the Quarter Sessions that gives a stark picture of the conditions there in 1858:

> "There are three cells, one for women and two for men, the largest of them 7ft 5in x 7ft 2in x 7ft 5in high.
> The ventilation is very imperfect owing to the increased number of prisoners continually under remand for trial, particularly under the Criminal Justice Act. There were at one time recently four prisoners confined in the smallest of these cells, sleeping in a bed 5ft 9in x 2ft 6in. There is no proper yard in which the prisoners can exercise.
> The privy is most offensive, and the close proximity of a yard for killing pigs and a horse-dung heap vitiate the air."

Here is a typical sample of inmates from Hertfordshire's bridewells, their offences and the sentences they were serving:

Year	Prisoner	Offence	Sentence
1674	William Bassill	"unlawfull coursing, killing, hunting and taking away one redde deare."	six months
1798	John Townsend	ill using his wife.	14 days
1806	Jemima Jones	wandering abroad and otherwise out in an idle and disorderly manner.	14 days hard labour
1827	George Jennings	running away and leaving his family as a burden on the parish of Harpenden.	one month
1832	James Gower	unlawfully attempting to take away and destroy fish from the reservoir.	14 days

1862	John Porter	being a rogue and vagabond at Caddington.	one month

Above: Berkhamsted Bridewell before its demolition in 1893. From a contemporary illustration. (author)

The bridewell at Hertford had been in Back Street (now Railway Street). It was in poor condition, and in 1789 the justices decided to build a new one next to their new prison in the Ware Road. The gaoler was also the keeper of the bridewell, so it made sense. The work was completed three years later. In 1820, the bridewell was fitted with a treadwheel for grinding corn. As a result of the increase in effort by the prisoners, their rations had to be improved. The justices then discussed whether the speed of the wheel should be increased. An interesting cycle - the more the prisoners worked, the more food they needed. But then, the more work they were given, so the more food they presumably needed...

Hertfordshire Gaols and Prisons

The earliest recorded gaols in Hertfordshire were in castles. Bishop's Stortford and Hertford are reasonably well documented, and there was a dungeon at Berkhamsted, though little is known about it; in the sixteenth century, Leland said that he "markid dyverse towers in the midle warde of this castelle and the dungeon hill..." It was thought in the 19th century that the dip in the centre of the castle mound was the remains of this dungeon. It is more likely that it was a well.

Later the county gaols at Hertford and St. Albans were established. Over the years they have occupied several buildings, some parts of which still stand.

Bishop's Stortford

The earliest mention of Bishop's Stortford being used as a prison seems to be in 1234, when a prisoner was held there charged with murder. Though used occasionally for criminals, this dungeon, known as the "Bishop's Hole" or the "Bishop's Prison," was principally used as an ecclesiastical gaol by the Bishops of London.

Conditions in the 14th century were wretched. The accused heretic Ranulf died whilst held there in 1336. In 1344 there were some fifty prisoners, and a further seven being locked up that year. Twenty-nine died. The following year, nine out of twenty-five died. The cost of keeping them was estimated to be a farthing per prisoner per day. Prisoners were shackled and chained, but it did not prevent them escaping. Batches of prisoners escaped year after year; it is possible that they were allowed to do so by sympathetic gaolers. William Grey, the bishop in 1429, was fined 640 marks by the king for allowing five prisoners to escape.

Right: a nineteenth century engraving, somewhat romanticised, of Thomas Pounde is put in irons at Bishop's Stortford prison (Picture source unknown).

During the reign of Mary I, between 1553-8, Bishop Bonner used the prison to hold Protestants, and under Mary's successor, Elizabeth, Catholics were held there, including Thomas Pound, or Pounde, in 1580.

The prison is only sketchily described. It was built of wood and brick, with a "deep and dark dungeon." On the other side of the moat from the keep, it survived longer than the castle itself, and was said in 1598 to be "a dungeon deep and strong." Pound described his cell as "a large vast room, cold water, bare walls, noe windows but loopholes too high to look out at, nor bed, nor bedsteade, nor place very fit for any but the homliest of stockes..." He referred to chains, fetters and urginalls (thumbscrews). The walls varied between three and five feet thick.

The building was demolished in 1649, and an inn called the Cherry Tree was built on the site. The inn was later incorporated into a building called Castle Cottage.

Many years later, human remains were found between the inn and the moat, in shallow graves. It was believed at the time, probably correctly, that they were all that was left of some of the prisoners who had died during their incarceration.

Hertford Castle
In 1225, the crown ordered the building of a gaol in Hertford, in addition to the castle dungeon. Whether this was done is not known, but it is the first specific mention of a prison there.

Just over eighty years later, the Knights Templar were imprisoned either at the castle or in prison in the town. The order had become powerful and very wealthy since their founding in about 1120. As a religious order, they paid no taxes, and had received a number of valuable bequests. By 1305 there were some 15,000 knights, controlling about 9,000 castles and manors throughout Europe. The charges of heresy brought against them at the instigation of Philip VI of France were a mixture of fact and fiction, but based on avarice. The Templars imprisoned at Hertford were from Temple Dinsley, near Hitchin. Other Templar possessions in Hertfordshire were at Baldock, Standon and Bengeo. There were only six members of the order in Temple Dinsley, and four of them were brought to Hertford and held for there for six months.

The next prisoners known at Hertford had a much easier time of it. Following the capture of David II of Scotland, he was held there between 1346 - 57. A good deal of freedom was allowed him, suggesting that he gave his parole. Only two years later, King John and Prince Philip of France were captured and held under similar conditions.

The Peasants' Revolt of 1381 saw some real prisoners at the castle. They were held in the dungeons near the main gate. They came from St. Albans, amongst them John Grindecobb. They were eventually returned to St. Albans, where some were executed.

James I of Scotland was the next royal prisoner. He was held for a total of 17 years, after being captured on his way to France.

Under Mary's persecution of the Protestants, Lawrence Parnam, a smith of Hoddesdon, was held at Hertford. There is a reference that in 1594 four prisoners escaped from "the gaol at the castle," but I am not convinced that it is authentic. There probably were prisoners after Parnam, but if so their names are now lost.

During the first half of the 17th century, the castle fell into decay, and the dungeon was used no more.

The Back Street Gaol, Hertford

Little is known of the Back Street gaol, not even when it was built; it is known that it was located near to the bridewell, however. The earliest record is from 1591. Several prisoners are recorded as having tried to escape in 1593 (three were successful).

In 1646 one of the inmates was Anthony Burchmore, who petitioned the Quarter Sessions for release. He had, he said, been in Hertford Gaol for some time, and was "naked and without parel." He had previously been at Aylesbury Gaol, where his clothes had become "full of filth and as good as all torn off."

By 1694 the gaol was reported to be in poor condition, and eight years later it was replaced by the gaol in Fore Street.

The Fore Street Gaol, Hertford

The new gaol opened in 1702, and met with problems almost from the start. Throughout its life it was overcrowded, and was hit by outbreaks of typhus and smallpox. The inhabitants of the town petitioned the justices for something to be done on several occasions. 1732: "...the prisoners in the gaol for the county of Hertford have... been frequently and very grievously afflicted with this infectious distemper called the gaol fever... and thereby many prisoners have lost their lives..." The petitioners expressed concern that the infection might spread to the town, and pointed out that the justices were likely to be infected too, reminding them of instances in the past when court officials had died as a result.

The building was constantly in need of repair, and insecure; there were escapes in 1739 and 1750. A new prison was built in the late 1770's, but not before John Howard had visited Fore Street:

> "The old gaol, built 1702, was in the middle of the town. In front two small day rooms, for felons, in which they were always locked up; no fireplace. Their dungeons or night-rooms, one down eighteen steps, the

other nineteen. Over their day rooms, was a large lumber room; and joining to it a lodging room for women felons. On each side of it were two rooms on the ground floor, and two chambers for debtors. No chapel, no infirmary. The Act for preserving the health of prisoners, and clauses against spirituous liquors, not hung up.

"In the interval of two of my visits gaol-fever prevailed, and carried off seven or eight prisoners, and two turnkeys. The felons were on that occasion removed to the Bridewell. At my second visit in 1776, four were sick."

As a footnote he says "I was well informed, that a prisoner brought out dead, from one of the dungeons, on being washed under the pump, showed signs of life, and soon after recovered. Since this, I have known other instances of the same kind."

The gaoler (Cornelius Willson) received no salary, only a flat rate of £39 6s. 10d. to supply bread to the felons. He held a licence to supply beer and wine to the prisoners, and charged fees and garnish.

Both Willson and the surgeon, Mr. Cutler, complained to the justices about the condition of the gaol and the unacceptable level of sickness in it. Eventually the decision was taken to build a new one. The old gaol was converted into tenements, but demolished not long afterwards, and a butchers' market built on the site.

The Ware Road Gaol, Hertford
Once the decision had been made, an Act of Parliament was required to proceed. This was passed in 1775. Several sites were considered for the new gaol, but the site finally selected was off the Ware Road. The land was bought for £500; the building cost £6,000.

Howard saw the new gaol on a later visit to Hertford, and was favourably impressed:

"[the] old gaol could not have been made healthy and convenient; but the prisoners are now in a new one situated just out of town, with separate wards (sixteen foot eight inches by eleven feet seven inches) and courts for debtors, men felons and women felons; the whole is properly surrounded by a wall fifteen feet high; which being at considerable distance from the building, the keeper has within a convenient garden.
The felons look healthy and well, which I am persuaded was owing to the gaoler's not crowding them into few rooms."

Given the manner in which gaol fever was spread, Howard was probably right. Built of brick, the new gaol comprised the following accommodation:

men debtors	ten cells and a large yard
women debtors	one cell and a yard
men prisoners	seventeen cells, four day rooms and four yards
women prisoners	three cells, one day room and two yards

The cells varied in size from 17ft square to 14ft by 12ft. A total of ten women and seventy men could be held at any one time.

However much more pleasant the new gaol was, it did not stop prisoners wanting to escape, and in 1780 two did so, causing some damage in the process. As a result the building was lined with York stone at a cost of £186. More got out in 1787, when £1 9s. 7d. was the cost of "planks, iron Bars etc., to make good the Hole in the wall where the prisoners broak threw." More money was spent on iron spikes to stop them going over the wall, and oak planks were laid to stop them burrowing beneath. A more secure cover to the well was fitted to prevent the more desperate of them from committing suicide.

The Session Rolls give an interesting insight into some of the costs of running a gaol in the 1790's:

whipping Thomas Baker	5s.
conveying John Savil and John Tyard to Ware and whipping them 150 yards	£1
conveying Sarah Gregory on board the *Lady Juliana* lying...below Woolwich (for transportation)	£1 16s.

The governor of the gaol was also the keeper of the bridewell. In 1790 he convinced the justices that the old bridewell in Back Street should close, and a new one be built in the Ware Road as a wing of the county gaol.

A report for 1818 gives the total number of committals as 178, with the highest number of prisoners at any one time as 24. The allowance was 1½ pounds of bread per day (additional rations had been given for six weeks, during an outbreak of typhus fever). Fires were allowed in the day rooms during the winter. A rug was provided for each bed.

The total number of committals two years later was 311, of which 52 were debtors; of the remaining 259, 115 had been tried, and 144 had not; 207 were men, 52 were women; and 15 were under seventeen years old, and 244 above.

In 1820 a treadwheel was installed. It was 50 ft long and 21 ft wide, with twenty-four steps 7½ inches apart. The hours worked varied with the seasons, from seven hours per day in the winter to nine hours in the summer months. The power generated was used to grind flour from coarse to fine.

In 1824 an act was passed creating a duty to preserve the health and improve the morality of inmates. Each prisoner should, if he could not have a cell to himself, at least have his own bed. The act was largely ineffective due to the reluctance of local authorities to enlarge their gaols or build new ones. There was of course no central body enforcing compliance.

Right: the window of the cell for condemned men at the Ware Road Gaol, Hertford. This is all that now remains of the buildings. (author)

In order to meet the requirements of the act as best they could, the Hertford justices ordered work to be carried out to keep different categories of prisoners apart. The categories identified were

- male debtors
- male prisoners convicted of a felony
- male prisoners convicted of a misdemeanour

- male prisoners committed on a charge or suspicion of a felony
- male prisoners committed on a charge or suspicion of a misdemeanour or for want of sureties
- female debtors
- female prisoners convicted or committed on a charge or suspicion of a felony
- female prisoners convicted or committed on a charge or suspicion of a misdemeanour or for want of sureties.

The notion that some form of education might benefit both the prisoners and society as a whole resulted in 1833 in the appointment of a schoolmaster for the juvenile offenders. By 1849 a Mr. Irving was teaching two hours a day, at a salary of £80 a year. The chaplain reported that the evening classes were well attended.

The expenses for the gaol for 1841 make interesting reading:

Salaries	Governor, Turnkeys & Watchmen		381	7	6
	Chaplain		200	0	0
	Surgeon		100	0	0
	Matron		15	0	0
	Clerk & Schoolmaster		42	0	0
Maintenance of Prisoners (inclusive of House of Correction)					
	Meat	ditto	57	11	5
	Bread	ditto	349	11	0
	Milk	ditto	45	2	7
	Groceries &c.	ditto	23	16	8
	Extras in Illness	ditto	2	3	4
Wood & Coals		ditto	45	14	0
Oil & Gas		ditto	24	19	1
Conveyance of Prisoners to Shire Hall for Trial			9	0	0
Conveyance of Prisoner to Hulks-Gaoler's Actual Expenses			23	0	2
Repair of Buildings			837	14	5
Rates and Taxes of the Governor's House & Offices			8	19	6
Stationery and Advertisements for Tenders			57	11	9
Postage & Carriage of Parcels			1	2	7
Sundries			12	9	1
Total			**2237**	**3**	**1**

Still the prisoners escaped; one in 1859, who was recaptured, and one in 1865, who was not.

Following the Prisons Act of 1877, many prisons closed across the country, especially those that could not be made to meet regulations. Could Hertford be modified to meet the requirements of the separate system, with every prisoner confined in a cell of his or her own? It could not. In 1878 the decision was made to close the Ware Road Gaol, and transfer the inmates to the more modern establishment at St. Albans.

The buildings were demolished a year later, though the chaplain's house stood until the 1930's. The only remnant is a grill mounted in a wall in Yeoman's Court. It is said to be the window of the condemned cell, which looked into the chaplain's garden.

St. Albans

As with the courts, the existence of the Liberty of St. Albans and the Borough complicated matters. Each had its own gaol, though they shared a bridewell. In 1867 a new gaol was built in Grimstone Road to house all prisoners, and not before time.

The Abbey Gatehouse, St. Albans - the Liberty Gaol, the Borough & Liberty Bridewell

The building dates at least from the 14th century, and form one of the most picturesque gaols imaginable. Conditions for the inmates did not correspond to the appearance of buildings however.

The eastern half (that nearest the abbey church) was the Liberty Gaol; the western side was the bridewell, shared by the borough and the liberty. As part of the Abbey, the gateway was originally the property of the Abbot of St. Albans. According to Howard, when he visited it in 1776 it was owned by Lord Salisbury. His report went on:

"For Debtors, two spacious day-rooms, and three lodging-rooms. - For Felons, three strong rooms. No court-yard: no water. Keeper, same as the Borough Gaol: Salary £16 : Fees £0 : 14 : 4, no Table [of fees]."

In a later edition of *The State of the Prisons* Howard refers to the felons' rooms as "offensive." Men and women could not be separated. A licence was held by the gaoler to supply beer. The gaoler was accused in 1800 of treating a prisoner so badly that he died shortly afterwards. He was dismissed as being quite unfit to be responsible for the care of those in gaol.

We have some idea of the number of prisoners, both from Howard in the late 18th century and the censuses of 1851 and 1861:

March 1776   no prisoners.
November 1776   1 debtor.

1779	1 felon.
1782	no prisoners.
1787	6 felons.
1851	42 prisoners (this total is for both gaol and the bridewell, and includes 11-year old Emma Fisher).

Above: the Abbey gatehouse at St. Albans. The gaol was in the east part of the building - the left side in this picture. The west side was the Bridewell. (author)

As elsewhere in Hertfordshire, the daily allowance was 1 pound of bread, rising to 1½ pounds after 1812. No allowance was given for heating, and it is said that the prisoners lowered a shoe on a piece of string in order to beg for coins to buy fuel (the shoe is on display in the Museum of St. Albans).

By 1794 prison labour was being used at the gaol to pump water, both for the gaol itself and the "poor inhabitants of the town." Both male and female prisoners were put to work on pumping.

From 1804, French prisoners of war joined the inmates. As POWs, their allowance of food was much better than the local prisoners. The gaoler's armoury was increased with a "small house gun with bayonet," presumably to help control these enemy captives.

The escape of George Pain in 1847 caused something of a stir, if only for its daring. He jumped from the top of the gatehouse into nearby trees, and made his way to the ground. Despite his injuries he got clear, and remained at large for six years, until recaptured in Leicester.

On the 1st November 1867, the inmates were transferred to the new gaol in Grimstone Road. The Hertfordshire Advertiser reported that at the old gaol it had not been possible to separate different categories of prisoner, and that

"the prison was a school of vice, in which inmates entertained each other with tales of villainy, and the invention of schemes of plunder and outrage to be carried into execution after release. Young offenders were obliged to be placed in the company of those old in sin, and the result may be easily imagined..."

The Borough Gaol, or Compter, in St. Albans Town Hall

The Town Hall was a 16th century timber frame building, and was used as the Borough court. The Compter was below, and used to hold petty offenders, felons, untried prisoners & debtors. Howard described the conditions in 1782:

"Debtors have sometimes the use of the town-hall in the day-time: the lodging-room of those that pay joins it. Felons and poor debtors have two day-rooms, and two close offensive night-rooms: no fireplace. Allowance for felons, a pound of bread a day. No straw: no court: no water. Fees for felons, 13s. 4d. Licence for beer... The debtors from the court of requests (debts under 40s.) are confined here with felons. Though the act of 25th. Geo. II. clears them in forty-two days, yet as it does not specify the gaoler's fee... they must continue in prison until they can pay whatever the gaoler demands."

The prison's population at Howard's visits was:

March 1776	no prisoners.
November 1776	2 debtors, 2 felons.
1779	no prisoners.
1782	1 debtors, 1 felon.
1787/8	1 felon.

By the early 19th century it was in poor condition, and all agreed that it needed to be replaced. The old building was demolished and the new one completed in 1831. There were two cells beneath the court, one for males and one for females.

The keeper of the gaol, James Deayton, was responsible for corporal punishment of offenders; he submitted a bill at the 1788 Michaelmas Quarter Sessions that included an item of 10s. for the public whipping of William Dick. At the same Sessions, Mary Twitchell, keeper of the bridewell, submitted a bill for 5s. for the private whipping of Thomas Saveall. It is interesting to speculate on the difference in amount. Was Deayton paid more because he was a man? Or perhaps the whipping of gaol inmates was more important than that of bridewell prisoners. Perhaps Dick received more lashes...

Grimstone Road, St. Albans

The Prisons Act of 1865 required the adoption of the separate system throughout the English prisons. None of the gaol buildings in St. Albans could be converted to meet this demand, so a new prison was designed and built in Grimstone Road. The building cost £14,000, though its regime did not conform strictly to the separate system, as we shall see. The Hertfordshire Advertiser described it in detail.

It was built of brick. Over the gateway was a portcullis, with the governor's house on one side, and the chief warden's accommodation on the other. A ventilation shaft 60 feet high rose above. There were 78 cells for men, and ten for women. Each cell was 12ft by 7ft, and 9 ft high. A small window gave "a not too cheerful light." Heating was by hot water pipes. Each cell had a gas light, which was controlled from the corridor outside. In the centre of each door was a spring-loaded "ration trap," and a glazed inspection hole. Water was rationed to nine gallons per day for all purposes. The prisoners slept in hammocks, which during the day were stowed on one of three slate shelves. Each cell was connected to a communication system, which allowed the inmates to call a prison officer.

There were waiting and retiring rooms, offices, bath and reception rooms, and a visiting justices' room.

On reception, prisoners were stripped and forced to bathe. Their clothes were fumigated, and they were issued with a prison uniform. There were two cells for prisoners with the "itch," and a dead house (mortuary). There were rooms for the surgeon and the chaplain, and rooms in the basement where prisoners worked under supervision (a modification to the separate system - in fact, very similar to the silent system). The kitchens, scullery and bakehouses were next to the store rooms. There were two punishment cells for solitary confinement, with double doors to ensure that no sound from the outside reached the prisoner.

The visiting room had three compartments, where on rare occasions prisoners could speak to friends and relatives. Similar rooms and arrangements existed for women.

The chapel separated male and female prisoners, whilst permitting the chaplain and guards to see them all (many prison chapels had single booths for prisoners, so that they could not even see other inmates, let alone talk to them. Getting the prisoners into the chapel could be a lengthy process, as each had to be placed in his stall before the next could enter the chapel).

The treadwheel had a capacity of 32, in divided compartments. Each revolution sounded a bell; after ten revolutions, the prisoners were allowed to rest (this was later changed to 20 minutes on the wheel, 10 minutes off). The treadwheel supplied the prison's water.

Above: the entrance to the Grimstone Road Gaol in St. Albans. (author)

The reporter found it gratifying that the prisoners "do not at all relish the change from the Old Gaol to the New." He went on to say that "... the care that is taken to conform to sanitary laws... is a positive source of discomfort... and gives them a still greater dread of prison discipline."

There was adequate capacity in the prison, at least to begin with, though the trend in numbers of prisoners was in line with the rest of the country - upwards. The census figures for 1871-91 were:

Year	Men	Women	additional details
1871	34	5	30 were from Hertfordshire.
1881	57	5	1 under 14.
1891	63	5	1 under 14. Two of the women recorded as prostitutes.

Executions were carried out in the prison, a black flag being flown at half-mast on the fateful day.

In 1901 when Mary Ansell was hanged at the gaol for murder, a crime to which another person is said to have later confessed. The last execution at St. Albans was that of George Anderson in 1914.

During the First World War Grimstone Road became a military prison. It was to see no more civilian inmates. Hertfordshire criminals henceforth served their time in other prisons - in 1915, for example, one of the Fox twins, the infamous poachers, was sent to Bedford Gaol.

The prison gatehouse still stands, as does part of the perimeter wall. The entrance is probably best known for its use in the opening sequences of the "Porridge" television series (other sequences were filmed at a malt house in Baldock, now destroyed by fire).

The prison itself is gone, and on the site are the offices of an insurance company. During redevelopment a curious, and as yet unexplained discovery was made: a cannon was recovered from 20ft below ground. It bore the date 1877, the number 85, and was apparently made by the Royal Ordnance Factory. The date does not however match the design, which is much earlier. It is now mounted in front of the gatehouse.

Transportation

Transportation of criminals was authorised by Parliament in 1597 by "an Act for the Punishment of Rogues, Vagabonds and Sturdy Beggars." The original destination was North America, where the transportees were sold as slaves to work on the plantations. The first transport ship left British waters in 1615.

Initially merchants carrying the transportees were paid according to the number of criminals carried from the shores of Britain. Following a high number of deaths amongst the cargo of the first vessels, the policy was changed. Payment was made for prisoners arriving alive. The mortality rate fell at once.

In many cases a sentence of transportation was given instead of the death penalty. The period could be for seven years or more, and was most often in multiples of seven; but other periods were specified, and it could also be for life. Keziah Little was transported for seven years by Hertford Assizes in 1757, as was John Abbey in 1770. Silvia and Rebecca Hicks got 14 years at the same assizes, and Thomas Horner got 21 years. Thomas and John Day were sent for life. Unfortunately their offences are not recorded in the transportation records. Little sailed aboard the *Thetis*, the rest on the *Thornton*.

The penalty for returning before the sentence was completed was death. In 1784 Peter Gibbons, a rat-catcher, reported that he had met a man named Joseph Ayre in St. Albans, "at the sign of the Valiant Trooper." Gibbons swore that he knew Ayre to have been transported for life at York for highway robbery eighteen years before. Ayre was arrested, but claimed that his name was not Ayre, but John Wainwright. He was held at the Borough Gaol for about a month before he disappears from the records. His fate is unknown; but as a complaint was sworn that he had been seen walking from the gaol to the King's Head alehouse and back, alone, during the period of his imprisonment, it seems that the gaoler at least had confidence in his innocence.

The American War of Independence brought an end to transportation to America after 1783, and presented the government with a serious problem. As a backlog of prisoners built up, alternatives were sought.

As a temporary expedient, old ships moored at Plymouth, Portsmouth, Sheerness, Chatham and Woolwich were employed to hold them. Conditions initially were very poor in every sense, but improved slightly as teething problems were ironed out. These prison hulks were never pleasant though, and several scandals broke over the years. Mortality rates aboard some vessels were high. These old ships were used as holding prisons for transportees for many years to come. The prisoners were "to be punished by being kept to hard labour in the raising of sand, soil & gravel, and cleansing the River Thames, or any other service for the benefit of the navigation of the said river." In fact they were also put to work on shore-based projects where the labour of many men was required.

A new destination was finally selected - Australia (and later, Tasmania, known at the time as Van Dieman's Land). The first fleet sailed in 1787, carrying 586 male and 192 female prisoners, along with some free settlers. They arrived in January 1788.

Above: the Discovery, *a prison hulk moored at Deptford in 1825. (from a contemporary engraving by Samuel Prout)*

Amongst them was James Freeman, sentenced to transportation for highway robbery in 1784, at the age of sixteen. Freeman became the first hangman in Australia. In 1788 he was caught stealing flour and was sentenced to death, but offered a pardon if he would hang Thomas Barrett, also found guilty of theft of rations. He also hanged Ann Davis, who in 1789 was the first woman executed in Australia.

The first woman from Hertfordshire to be transported was Sarah Gregory, who stole four pigs worth £6 in St. Albans. She took her eight-year-old daughter with her.

Over 1,300 prisoners from Hertfordshire were transported from Hertfordshire - here are just a few:

Name	Year	Town of Origin	Sentence	Offence
Thomas Pateman	1789	North Mimms	7 yrs	theft of 500 pounds of lead from the roof of the church at South Mimms.
William Ambrose	1794	Hemel Hempstead	7 yrs	theft of a pig.
Esther Absalom	1807	Chipping Barnet	7 yrs	theft of a linen sheet worth 2s.
William Fish	1820	Bishop's Stortford	life	theft of a watch worth 10s.
William Andrew	1828	Stapleford	7 yrs	poaching.
Frederick Everett	1836	Offley	7 yrs	theft of 200 tame pigeons.
William Walsh	1836	Oxford	14 yrs	theft of a hat at Northchurch, worth 5s., and a handkerchief.
James Osbourne	1848	Little Hadham	life	aiding in the rape of Mary Warman.

The last vessel to carry transportees was the *Hougoumont*, in 1867, bound for Western Australia. During the history of transportation, some 40,000 prisoners were sent to America and 162,000 to Australasia - 202,000 in all. Of those sent to Australia, only 1,303 were from Hertfordshire.

Not all those sentenced to be transported were actually sent overseas - some served their sentence at home, in convict prisons or on the hulks; others were given the option of joining the army instead; and some were pardoned.

Other forms of Punishment

Fines and Atonement
The imposition of fines is an early form of punishment, which, together with a system of atonement, formed a major part of the legal structure in Anglo-Saxon times.

Fines were known as *wite* or *wita*, and were punishments in the form of monetary payment as we understand fines today. Atonement, or *bot,* was a payment to the victim of the crime or his heirs to compensate them for their loss. The nearest parallel today is an award of damages, but before the Norman Conquest it extended to include crimes of violence, including murder. By paying a man's *wer-gild* to his kin, the crime could be settled.

Anglo-Saxon fines were carefully graded according to the status of the offender. The more important he was, the more he paid. Some of the legal codes consist of little more than lists of fines.

Fines became less common under the Normans. As a general rule, it was felt that they should not exceed the offender's ability to pay - a principle reinforced by Magna Carta: "They [the fines] are not to be so heavy, in the case of grievous crimes, as to deprive any man of his means of livelihood."

In the succeeding centuries the gallows and whip ruled, though fines were occasionally levied, as can be seen from earlier chapters. From the mid-Victorian period however they began to dominate to a greater and greater degree, a trend which has continued. Should the offender be unable to pay the fine, the alternative has often been a period of imprisonment or a flogging.

Fines have varied from as little as 1d. to substantial sums, depending upon the offence and the offender. Some of the early fines were quite heavy. From the Laws of King Alfred, circa 890 AD: "If a man fight before a king's ealdorman in the *gemot*, (meeting) let him make *bot*... (atonement) and *wite* (pay a fine), as it may be right; and before this, 120 shillings to the ealdorman as *wite*. If he disturb the *folkesmote* by drawing his weapon, 120 shillings to the ealdorman as *wite*. If aught of this happen before a king's ealdorman's junior, or a king's priest, 30 shillings as *wite*."

From 1914 offenders were given time to find the money to pay fines, and allowed to pay by instalments - both major steps in reducing prison populations.

Outlawry
We tend to interpret the word "outlaw" as meaning a criminal on the run. Originally it meant that and somewhat more.

An outlaw in the Anglo-Saxon period was literally a person outside the law. His goods were subject to confiscation. He could not expect the protection of the law, or assistance from society in any way. He was fair game. An outlaw could be robbed, assaulted or even killed by anyone who felt like it without reprisal. He could not sue in the courts, but he could be sued. He could no longer rely on help from his friends - if they were caught helping him, they could be subject to the same penalty themselves. To be declared an outlaw was, then, a serious a matter; in fact it could be a matter of life or death.

Later, outlawry was used to force people to appear in court. Should they fail to appear, their goods were subject to confiscation, and they were subject to unlimited imprisonment.

The procedure was as follows: demands for appearance were made in five Hundred (County) Courts in succession via a *writ exigent*. Failure to appear resulted in a declaration of outlawry.

For example, a *writ exigent* was issued against, amongst others, John Carter of Furneaux Pelham and Agnes Newman of Buntingford on 10 May 1590. The proclamations were made in the Hundred Courts of Buntingford on 11 June, Hoddesdon on 9 July, Ware on 6 August, Hatfield on 3 September, and Buntingford again on 1 October. Agnes Newman did not appear, and was therefore outlawed. John Carter turned up, and so the writ against him was cancelled.

Outlawry was used until the 18th century, when John Wilkes, the political agitator, was outlawed in 1764. He fled to France, but on his return the writ against him was found to be flawed; though it is likely that whatever had happened some reason would have been found to acquit him, as he was by then a member of parliament. Trying him would have had considerable political implications.

Outlawry was never used again, but it remained on the statute books until the Administration of Justice Act of 1938.

The Stocks and the Pillory

Both the stocks and the pillory had the same aim - to expose an offender to humiliation, ridicule and abuse. In some cases unpleasant and often dangerous objects were thrown at the occupants. There were instances of people in the pillory or stocks being killed.

The offender condemned to the stocks sat with their feet, and sometimes their hands as well, trapped in a wooden frame. The pillory held the wrists and neck, with the offender standing. In both cases, the restriction of movement for a prolonged period caused intense pain.

Both forms of punishment were, then, far more serious than the modern image of them as a quaint old custom; that of the pillory or stocks on the village green, with over-ripe tomatoes as ammunition, and so on.

There is reason to believe that little distinction is made between the two in the records before the 17th century. Most records refer to the pillory, but the survivors of such implements of punishment in Hertfordshire are all stocks.

That pillories existed is undoubted, as there are contemporary references to them. Examples remain in other parts of the country, however, and they show a wide variety of design. Some, like that illustrated below, consist of a single upright with the restraining timbers mounted on its top. Others have two uprights, with the cross pieces between them – rather like a set of inverted stocks with long uprights. Such a pillory can be found in Saffron Walden Museum in Essex. Records show that some were constructed to hold one person, others for as many as twelve. Examples were even made that rotated, so that the offender could be turned to face all parts of the crowd.

Above: the stocks at Aldbury. Note the fittings on the left-hand post; this stocks, like many others, combines a whipping post. (author)

There was some variety in the construction of stocks. Some catered for several people - usually not more than three - whilst others were fitted with a whipping post at one end. The lower section of the stocks was fixed; the upper section was either hinged or moved in a slot to allow the offender's feet and sometimes hands into the holes. Pillories worked in a similar manner. In Hertfordshire they all seem to have been made of wood, but stone uprights were used for stocks in some parts of the country - there is an example at Chapel-en-le-Frith in Derbyshire, one of several in that county.

The period of confinement varied - it might be one hour, or many hours. The penalty for drunkenness in the 1620's was a fine of 3s. 4d. or 4 hours in the stocks (later increased to 5s. or 6 hours). In 1541 John Gelly was placed in the stocks at St. Albans from one hour before to one hour after the market, though his offence is unrecorded.

Here are a few examples of the use of the pillory and stocks in Hertfordshire:

1579   Alice Cowle of Therfield, indicted for witchcraft. She bewitched a brewing vat full of water from which two cows were drinking. She was sentenced to be pilloried four times for the space of six hours, and to confess her offence.

1600   an order to the constables of Ashwell, from the justices at Hertford: "all such poor inhabitants of Ashwell as are taken breaking hedges, or stealing, or cutting down wood, that for every such offence so committed the men and women for the first offence to be stocked, except the women at the time of the fact committed be great with child; children to be whipped for same offence."

1697   Philip Dugard of Bishop's Stortford. Set in the stocks for "swearing two oaths," as he could not pay the 2s. fine.

1802   from John Carrington's diary: "Tuesday 18 (May) To Ware on poney, saw the Woman Stand in the pillery at Magpye Corner at Ware for almost starving a girll about 7 years old to Death, it was her husbands Child, She was mother in Law [step-mother]..."

The parish constable, or the community as a whole, was responsible for maintenance of the pillory and stocks. They were repaired or replaced as required. Hertford had its stocks repaired in 1633, and new sets in 1660 and 1773. The job was not always done properly: the stocks of Baldock were reported in 1575 to be "ruinous... the residents and inhabitants ... shall well and sufficiently repair them before the next court..."

Punishment was often on market days, and the stocks or pillory of market towns were usually sited in the market place, with the intention that the miscreants should be seen by as many people as possible. In Hertford they are shown on a map of 1766 on the east of the Market Place. Both St. Albans and Hitchin had their stocks in the Market Place too. In Royston, the pillory was near the stone cross.

Above left: a pillory. The prisoner was exposed to missiles hurled by the populace. There were instances of people being killed in the pillory. Right: the whipping post on Datchworth Green as it appeared in about 1900. It is now enclosed and fitted with a lead cap to protect it from the elements. (author)

The constable had the task of confining offenders in them, for which he was allowed a fee of 1s. Where there was no cage available, the stocks may also have been used by the constable to restrain prisoners, though a nearby inn was more likely.

By the year 1810, when David Maitland was pilloried for fraud at Hertford, "opisite the Angell Inn," use of the pillory was already in decline. It is said that the pillory was last used in Hertfordshire in 1812, when James Deaven was put in the pillory at St. Albans for an "unnatural assault." By 1816 the only remaining offence for which the pillory could be used was perjury. The stocks and pillory were formally outlawed by Act of Parliament in 1837. Though their use as a mode of punishment had long gone, in Berkhamsted in the mid 19th century the boys of Bourne School used to put new boys, and those leaving, in the stocks as a joke.

As with village cages, there is an enduring legend with stocks. They are said to have been burned on Guy Fawkes' night, on a bonfire.

A few stocks still exist, though in some cases they are reproductions. Some restoration has been carried out on the others, so that none can be said to be truly original. Aldbury stocks, on the village green, incorporates a whipping post, as does the stocks at Brent Pelham, just outside the churchyard (this is the best-preserved set in the county). Great Amwell's stocks were, in 1899, just below the church. They were moved into the churchyard, but in 1953 were reported to be no more than the "fast decaying remnants." Some restoration work has been done since then. The horizontal timbers have been replaced, and lead caps put on the uprights. There is no indication that the uprights, which stand 56 inches above ground, ever had the restraints of a whipping post.

Cucking Stools and Ducking stools

Despite the similarity in the name, cucking stools and ducking stools were different methods of punishment.

The cucking stool was a chair, similar to a commode in appearance. Its name reflects the similarity, coming as it does from *cukken*, meaning to defecate. The Anglo-Saxons used a comparable device for the punishment of scolds, called a scealding stool, and the cucking stool probably descended from it. The name was certainly used as long ago as the 13th century, and it is claimed that the town of Chester had such a chair at the time of Domesday. The stool was carried or wheeled around the community with the offender sitting in it, bare headed and footed, exposing him or her to abuse and ridicule. It was used for minor offences, especially scolds, and offenders against the Assize of Bread and Ale. Its use declined during the 16th century.

The cucking stool at Hertford is recorded as having been repaired in 1685, and in Baldock, at the same time as the stocks were reported to be in poor condition, the cucking stool also needed attention.

The ducking stool arrived somewhat later, in the early 17th century. It consisted of a chair attached to one end of a long pole, which was pivoted like a see-saw, so that the chair could be ducked into a pond or river ("duck pond" may refer to this use of a pool, and have nothing to do with waterfowl). Some ducking stools were fixed, others had wheels. In some cases the whole apparatus was backed into the water. There are records, though not in Hertfordshire, of ducking stools being used as late as the early 19th century.

Unfortunately neither cucking nor ducking stools have survived in Hertfordshire.

The Scold's Bridle

The scold's bridle was a brutal device for punishing women convicted of being scolds. It covered the head, and a rough tongue projected into the mouth of the offender, causing pain if the wearer tried to speak. Though there are several scold's bridles still in existence, unfortunately none are in Hertfordshire. The one pictured is in Morpeth. Another good example is in the possession of the Tower of London.

As minor offenders, scolds commonly appeared before a local magistrate, or the Court Leet if such existed in the area. An alternative punishment was the pillory or a fine. In 1467 Margaret, wife of Thomas Moss, Margaret, wife of

Richard Moss, and Mabel Tooby were convicted of being "common scolds." They were fined 3d., but they were warned that if they did not reform they would have to pay the lord of the manor 20d., with the threat of the pillory waiting in the wings.

Right: the scold's bridle. This example is in Morpeth Museum in Northumberland. It is placed over the head, and the spur fits into the unfortunate wearer's mouth. It is roughened to make talking painful, if not impossible. (author)

Corporal Punishment - Birching, Whipping and Flogging

Whipping and flogging have their roots in antiquity. They were firm favourites of the Romans, amongst others. The Anglo-Saxons punished some offences with a whipping, but for the most part they relied on fines or atonement.

Systematic whipping began following the notorious "Whipping Act" of 1530, which decreed that vagrants should be taken to the nearest town with a market place, stripped, tied to a cart's tail and flogged "until their back be bloody." The requirement that the offender be naked was amended in 1597, when it was decreed that they should be stripped to waist level only.

Whipping became popular with justices as an appropriate punishment for many offences, as the following examples testify:

1690   Moses Dunkly of Hunsdon, for stealing a shirt worth 6d. and stockings worth 2d. Sentenced to be whipped until his back be bloody at the Angel Inn Yard, Hertford.

1692   Elizabeth Ashwood, an "idle person," who broke into a house in Stondon and broke many of the windows. Sentenced to a moderate whipping.

1732   John Kilby of Bushy, for stealing an iron tobacco box, value 10d. Ordered to be "whipt at Hertford openly till his back be bloody, between the hours of 11 and 1 in the forenoon."

1742   Sara Ashby of Hemel Hempstead, whipped at the House of Correction for the theft of one small fish and a pint of beans.

1756   Rachel Bigg, of Little Ayot, who stole two ducks. She was sentenced to be "whipped from the Old Cross in Hertford through Maidenhead Street and the Butcher's Market to the Gaol, and to suffer the same next Saturday fortnight." The bill from Cornelius Willson, the gaoler, for carrying out the flogging was 10s.

1758   Robert Hammond of Stevenage, whipped for the theft of a pewter basin.

1769   Joshua Mead, of Harpenden, for running away and leaving his family chargeable to the parish: six months imprisonment at Hertford, and twice publicly whipped.

The whipping might be carried out by the parish constable, the hangman, or the keeper of the gaol or bridewell. Costs varied - anything from 2s. 6d. to 10s.

Whipping on the cart's tail eventually died out, being replaced by whipping at a post. Most communities had a whipping post, either as part of the stocks or standing alone. Few of the latter exist - only Datchworth has one in Hertfordshire. It is surrounded by railings, and has a lead cap to provide a degree of protection from the elements. Waltham Cross museum, just over the border, has a fine ornately carved whipping post dated 1598.

George Jeffreys, the 17th century judge famous for his brutality, was a staunch supporter of the whip. In one case he is quoted as saying to the hangman, "I charge you to pay particular attention to this lady. Scourge her soundly, man: scourge her till her blood runs down! It is Christmas, a cold time for madam to strip. See that you warm her shoulders thoroughly." He sentenced another victim to be flogged in every town in Dorset every year for seven years. The total number of floggings would have reached 182 during the period of the sentence, or once every two weeks. Jeffreys was the extreme, but others used the whip quite freely.

Whipping of women in public became less common from the 18th century, but whether women were flogged in public or the privacy of the bridewell was up to the local authorities. In some cases it made little difference - those with a taste for such spectacles bribed unscrupulous keepers to be allowed to watch the punishment being administered.

In 1792 whipping for female vagrants was abolished and in 1817 the public flogging of women was ended. Just three years later corporal punishment for women was abolished completely.

The last public flogging in Hertfordshire is reported to have been in 1838, whilst the last recorded use of the Datchworth post was on 27 July 1665, for the flogging of two vagabonds.

In 1861, whipping was abolished for all offences other than shooting at the sovereign and men convicted of vagrancy (though the birching of children continued). It was reintroduced however in 1863, by the so-called "Garotters' Act," and offenders were flogged once more, and with vigour. A period was allowed for the offender to recover between floggings, so that the punishment was sometimes delivered in instalments.

Flogging sentences became less common as the 19th century progressed, and were confined to a small number of justices. In the two years 1898/9, only five judges in the whole of England sentenced offenders to be flogged, on a total of 64 occasions. Of those, 35 were ordered by one judge, 16 by another, 9 by a third, and 3 and 1 by the remaining two. The sentences were for between 10 and 25 lashes.

In 1933 there were 49 floggings, only three years before a Commons Committee reported that it was "essentially an unconstructive punishment." In 1948 birching and flogging was abolished except for male prisoners guilty of serious disciplinary offences. Flogging continued in English prisons until the middle of the 20th century, before being finally abandoned in 1967. The tools most commonly used were the birch and the cat o' nine tails.

The birch consisted of a bundle of thin branches, bound together at one end to form a grip. In some cases it was soaked in water or vinegar before use. Its use on young offenders continued well into the twentieth century, though its decline was rapid; from about 5,000 in 1917 to 218 in 1935. In 1947 there were only 25, and those ordered by only two or three magistrates' courts.

Above: the birch. This example is for use on juvenile offenders. (author)

Law and Disorder in Hertfordshire

The punishment for offenders aged 8 to 16 years was six strokes, administered by a police constable, in private. The child received a medical examination before receiving the punishment, which was applied to the bare buttocks, and the doctor also examined him between strokes. The doctor had the power to discontinue the punishment at any time. A parent or guardian had the right to be present.

The cat o' nine tails was used for serious offences, and latterly for over 18 years old offenders only. By the start of the 20th century, floggings were formalised. The ends of the tails were whipped with silk, not knotted as they had been in the past. As with birching, a doctor was present, and had the power to stop the punishment. The neck and kidneys were protected, and the prisoner's view screened so that he could not see who was administering the punishment.

Judicial Mutilation

Mutilation is another ancient punishment. In most cases it consisted of branding or the cropping of ears, though in early days limbs were sometimes amputated.

In the late 15th century, ear cropping was most commonly used on vagrants, but it could be ordered for other offences as well. The Session Rolls record that Thomas Kent of Aston, struck Thomas Bettes, also of Aston, in the chancel of Hitchin church, drawing blood. He was therefore liable under statute to having his ears cropped, or being branded on the cheek.

Cropping continued to be used until the 17th century, when a case is recorded in London of a maid who gave poison to her mistress having both her ears cropped, and being branded on the brow.

In 1589/90 we have cases of "rogues" in Hertfordshire being branded in the right ear with an iron the breadth of a thumb. Branding was more commonly on the inside of the left hand; rogues and vagabonds being marked with an 'R', thieves with a 'T', those convicted of manslaughter with an 'M'. For theft from a shop however, the brand was on the cheek, and for perjury, a 'P' was branded on the forehead.

In the 17th century, branding and ear-cropping were most often used as punishments for forgery, perjury and libel. Blasphemers sometimes had their tongues bored through with a red hot poker.

Later cases of branding were of those granted benefit of clergy, so that they might not make a second claim. They were to be branded on the thumb in open court to ensure that there could be no avoiding retribution should they re-offend. There are two examples from Hertfordshire as late as 1766:

> Mary Gray   of Wideford, spinster, was burned in the hand in open court for theft of goods totalling 3s. 4d.

George Arnold   of Stevenage, labourer, for theft of a cloth greatcoat, value 2s. 6d., burned in the hand.

In both cases the value of the goods exceeds 1s., and their offences would have been grand larceny, which carried the death sentence. As they were branded, they must have claimed benefit of clergy.

Other forms of mutilation occurred, but these were incidental to the main purpose - the torture of the prisoner, either to extract information or a confession.

Capital Punishment

The main methods of execution in England have been hanging, beheading, drawing and quartering, burning and, for military personnel, shooting. Variations on these themes have also been tried. None have been truly humane, and arguably it is impossible to imagine a means of capital punishment that is so. Whether or not death or unconsciousness comes quickly, the anticipation of it must in most cases be a form of suffering difficult to comprehend.

Hanging

Hanging has been in use in England for longer than any other form of execution, and, as the method of capital punishment for the ordinary people, has accounted for the most deaths. Early hangings were a far cry from the almost scientific methods used in the mid 20th century. The hangman might even be the person who brought the prosecution, and with no experience at all. Sometimes the bailiff was tasked with finding a hangman. Larger towns might have a hangman appointed, but it would probably not be his main line of work. As late as 1800 at Gallows Hill in Hertford a man named Waters (alias Munt) was executed for robbery by an amateur - "wen they com to the gallows their was no Hangman and the man (Waters) had som hopes, but the Gaylor (Gaoler) made his Man Do the Job." Waters was the last man hanged on Gallows Hill, but he was not the first. The site had been used since 1741. The bodies of the executed prisoners were buried on the spot, where their bones were found much later by workmen digging for gravel.

The offender was forced up a ladder, a rope was put around his neck, and the hangman twisted the ladder. The criminal was said to have been "turned off." He was left to strangle at the end of the rope for between 30 minutes and an hour. Sometimes friends and relatives were allowed to relieve his suffering by pulling on his legs, thus hastening his death.

With a high profile execution, the hangman often earned extra money by selling sections of the rope, or fragments of the dead man's clothes, as souvenirs. Superstitious folk believed that by touching the body of a hanged man they could cure blemishes such as warts and pimples; the hangman could make money on that too.

Above: the public hanging of John Thurtell in Hertford, in 1824. It is said that the executioner was drunk. Thousands attended the hanging. From a contemporary pamphlet.

There were occasions, already mentioned, when bodies handed over for dissection were found still to be alive, and were revived. In the first half of the 19th century the procedure changed and executed prisoners were always buried in unconsecrated ground. It is therefore likely that some of them were buried alive.

The trap was introduced in 1783 at Newgate. The prisoner stood on a trapdoor while the executioner put the rope around his neck. The trap was released, and if all went well the prisoner's neck was broken and he died quickly. It was a long time before the trap spread through the country, and longer still before accurate tables were drawn up, giving the appropriate "drop" for the prisoner's height and weight. On one occasion in 1885 at Norwich the drop was too great and the unfortunate prisoner's head was pulled off. The hangman was James Berry. Perhaps more unfortunate were those given too short a drop - they would strangle, just like in the good old days.

By the time St. Albans Gaol closed, hanging had become a job for the professionals, who prided themselves on the speed with which they could get the condemned from his cell and end his life.

How much did an execution cost? In the case of William Salmon, hanged in 1795, it was

Horse and cart	11s.
rope and executioner	11s. 6d.
wine for sacrament	1s. 3d.
digging grave	2s.
Total	**£1 5s. 9d.**

Hangings were held in public until 1868. The populace were supposed to be deterred by the spectacle of justice in action; most went in ghoulish fascination. Hangings were immensely popular, with thousands attending, and high prices were paid for a good view. Sometimes the hanging was held at the gaol, or on a local gallows. In 1794, following the collapse of the old gallows at Hertford, a new, moveable scaffold was built. Criminals could now be executed close to the scene of their crime: the highwayman Robert Snooks was hanged and buried at Boxhill. He had robbed the post-boy there of six leather post bags in 1801. The same gallows were taken to a field near the home of Mr. and Mrs. Nathaniel Camp, who lived between Stanstead and Hunsdon, and used to execute the two men (W. Criswell and James Burgess) who had broken in and beaten and robbed them.

The last public execution at the Ware Road Gaol in Hertford was in 1839. After that they were held behind closed doors, the last being in 1876. When the Hertford Gaol closed, the centre of execution moved to St. Albans. By then however an execution was a rarity rather than the commonplace event it had been only sixty or seventy years before.

William Caldercraft between 1829-74 was on a retainer of one guinea a week, plus one guinea per execution. In 1884 James Berry was paid 10 guineas per hanging.

Hanging in Chains

Once the hanging had taken place, the body was sometimes hung up in a metal frame until it finally decomposed, which could take a year or more. The tradition dates from the Anglo-Saxon period, though in those days no iron frame was used; interments of Anglo-Saxon criminals are frequently found with the lower legs and arms missing due to decomposition. The intention was to provide a further deterrent to potential offenders. The face was sometimes covered, and the body left clothed. The inhabitants of St. Albans were forbidden to remove the remains of executed rebels after the Peasants' Revolt of 1381. It took fourteen months for them to decay.

Many years later, in the mid 18th century, the son of Mrs. Gatward, landlady of the Red Lion in Royston, was hanged for highway robbery, and left hanging in chains. After two or three months the body fell, and according to tradition, was buried by Mrs Gatward in the cellar of the inn. It has been suggested that young Gatward was suspended from Caxton Gibbet, now at the junction of the A1198 and the A428 in Cambridgeshire. A gibbet still stands at the crossroads, though it may not be original.

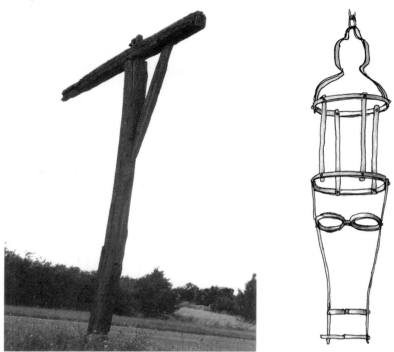

Above left: Caxton Gibbet, in Cambridgeshire. It is doubtful whether this is the original gibbet, though the timbers show signs of age. No gibbet survives in Hertfordshire. (author). Right: a set of chains for suspending the bodies of executed criminals. (author)

It has been suggested that at one time prisoners "convicted of wilful murther" were hanged in chains whilst still alive, and left to die of thirst and hunger. If so the evidence is very sparse, and I have come across no such cases in Hertfordshire.

Drawing and Quartering
The procedure is best described by the official record of a trial for high treason in 1685:

"You must, every one of you, be had back to whence you came, from thence you must be drawn to the place of execution, and there you must severally be hanged by the necks, every one of you by the neck till you are almost dead; and then you must be cut down, your entrails must be taken out and burnt before your faces, your several heads to be cut off, and your bodies divided into four parts, and these to be disposed of at the pleasure of the King; and the Lord have mercy on your souls."

Later the offender was allowed to die during the hanging phase of the proceedings, before disembowelling. Later still he was hanged then merely decapitated.

In the 17th century the form of words was "drawn, hanged and quartered." "Drawn" referred to the manner in which the victim was dragged to the place of execution on a hurdle or sledge, and not the disembowelling as is popularly believed.

John Ball, one of the leaders of the Peasants' Revolt of 1381 in Hertfordshire, was sentenced to be drawn on a hurdle, hanged, decapitated, disembowelled, and cut into quarters. It would seem that the judge was merciful in decapitating Ball before disembowelment, or perhaps the records are in error.

Beheading

Above: traitors' heads on display over London Bridge in the 16th century. From a nineteenth century engraving.

Execution by beheading was usually reserved for important prisoners and the aristocracy. Heads were sometimes displayed on London Bridge - several are visible in a panorama of London dated 1616. In many cases the heads were removed for display after the offender was hanged.

In early beheadings a heavy sword was used, later to be replaced by an axe. If the blow was struck cleanly, decapitation was quite a quick method of execution (though Mary Queen of Scots' eyes were said to have rolled, and her lips writhed, after her head was struck off). Unfortunately, either through nervousness or lack of experience, the headsman sometimes took several blows to end the prisoner's suffering.

The last beheading was in 1747, when Lord Lovat was executed for his part in the 1745 Rebellion.

Right: the headsman's block and axe, from a nineteenth century engraving of the equipment in the Tower of London.

Burning to Death

Contrary to popular belief, witches in England were not burned to death. Burning was reserved for a small number of offences, including heresy, and, for women, treason and petty treason. When witches were executed, they were hanged; though there is a record that a 10th century woman was drowned in London for making an image of Aelsi, son of Wulfstan, and driving nails into it.

Following the death of Edward VI in 1553, the Catholic Queen Mary took the throne. There followed a period of persecution of Protestants, and some 300 were burned for heresy. William Hale was burned at Barnet, and George Tankerville was executed in the same manner in an open space in front of St. Albans Abbey Gatehouse, now the graveyard. According to Chauncy, writing at the end of the 17th century, a third unnamed Protestant was burned at Bishop's Stortford, near the gaol.

In 1666 the wife of Robert Toefield was burned at Hertford for poisoning him, the crime being petty treason (the parish register of Berkhamsted records that Toefield was buried on 17 March. The entry is annotated "poysoned by his wife, burnt alive at Hertford"). This penalty for women was eventually abolished in 1790.

In the early days, the prisoner was burned alive whilst still conscious. By the time of Queen Mary, the prisoner was burned naked, but was permitted to have a bag of gunpowder tied around his neck to hasten his death; though it must have been agonising before the flames reached the bag.

The last burning was in 1789, by which time the victim was strangled before the pyre was lit.

Torture

Torture has never been a legal practice under English Common Law. As a result, its existence has sometimes been denied.

In fact it has been used, though normally authorised at the highest level - the Privy Council, or even the King. It seems always to have been considered a shameful custom however, and was usually carried out in secret. In 1606 Guy Fawkes was racked under a warrant signed by James I, who also authorised the scandalous torture of Sir Walter Raleigh. Fifty years later the law was changed so that only confessions freely given were admissible in court.

The commonest methods of torture were the rack, the scavenger's daughter and devices for crushing parts of the hands and feet (thumbscrews and the boots).

The rack stretched the victim; unfortunately no complete examples still exist, and contemporary illustrations are thought to be conjectural.

An example of the scavenger's daughter belonging to the Tower of London still exists. It looks innocuous, but it is an extremely brutal device that constricts the prisoner into a ball. It is reported that blood sometimes oozed from the ends of the fingers, or that the chest burst and blood flowed from the mouth.

Thumbscrews are almost self-explanatory: they were used to crush the thumbs. The boot was a large metal device that covered the leg from the knee down. Wedges were then hammered in between the boot and the flesh. The results can be imagined.

One other form of torture was used quite commonly, but for a different purpose from the others. Known as *peine forte et dure*, its purpose was to force prisoners to plead. If they did not plead, they could not be tried, thus escaping justice. First the threat, then the actuality of the torture was carried out.

In 1654 the procedure was described in detail:

> "...hee stands mute & refuseth to plead therefore hee must be sent to the prison from whence hee came & put into a meane house stopped from

light & there must bee layed uppon the bare ground wth out any litter straw or other Covering & wth out any garment about him saving something to cover his privy members & that hee must lye upon his backe & his head must bee Covered & his feete bare & that one of his armes shal be drawne wth a Cord to one side of the house & the other arme to the other side & that his leggs shalbe used in the same manner & that upon his body must be layed soe much yron & stone as he can beare & more & that the first day after hee must have three morsels of barley bread wth out any drinke. And the seconde day hee must drinke soe much as hee can three tymes of the water wch is next the prison dore saving running water wth out any bread & this must bee his dyett until hee dye."

Right: instruments of torture from the Tower of London, from a nineteenth century engraving. On the left is the scavenger's daughter. Next to it is a type of leg irons called bilboes. Below is an iron collar. It is filled with lead to make it heavier. It appears in an inventory of 1547 as a "stele color for a prysonr."

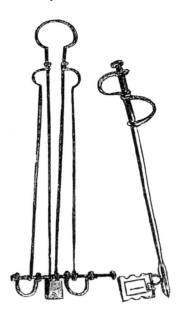

Right: the thumbscrews. The victim's thumbs were inserted by the torturer and the screw tightened. (author)

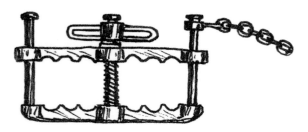

In 1603 Michael Deanes of Colney, a labourer, was indicted at Hertford for grand larceny. He was accused of stealing a dun gelding valued at 40s. and a pack of woollen cloth valued at the substantial sum of £61 from James Byrche. The record shows that he "stood mute; put to *peine forte et dure*." In 1611, Thomas Polyn stood mute at Hertford Assizes when accused of burglary. *Peine forte et dure* for him too. Why these men refused to plead, when the alternative was certain death is not clear. The most likely reason is to avoid bills of *attainder* or *corruption of the blood*. Attainder meant that the accused was disgraced and could have his property forfeited; corruption of the blood incurred the loss of inheritance. If the accused believed that conviction was certain, he could by refusing to plead ensure that his property passed to his dependants. An alternative reason might have been that they had been told that if they refused to plead they could not be tried, without being informed of the consequences. If so, this is an extreme case of a little knowledge being a dangerous thing. *Peine forte et dure* was discontinued in 1772.

Judicial torture was not strictly speaking a form of punishment. It was usually part of the trial process, with the punishment for the offence still to come. Also to be borne in mind is that the definition of torture has changed. In the second half of the 20th century, sleep deprivation, the withholding of food and drink and such methods were redefined as torture. This was certainly not the case in earlier times, and such techniques were used on terrorist suspects in Northern Ireland as late as the 1970's.

Chapter Four

Enforcement

The law has no effect if it is not enforced. Methods of law enforcement in England have improved considerably over the years, though none has been completely successful; but then, no country can lay claim to such perfection. Prosecution must always depend for example upon the identification of a suspect, and secret and apparently motiveless crimes present considerable difficulties to the investigator.

The Anglo-Saxons: Kin, Guilds and Frankpledge

In the early Anglo-Saxon period, peacekeeping was based on a system of kinship. Members of a kindred, or family, were jointly responsible for the maintenance of law and order. This system gave way to guilds, with shared responsibility for crimes and the support of guild members.

Both these systems of enforcement relied upon mutual accountability. Each member of the group, whether kinship or guild, was responsible for the behaviour of the others, and was liable for *bot* and *wer* in the offender's place should he fail to meet his obligations.

In addition, there was a system of sureties called *bohr*. Should the accused fail to appear before the court, the surety was forfeited.

By the 10th century all the makings of a new system were in place. Called *frankpledge*, it was to last more than 300 years.

Frankpledge seems to have evolved over the next hundred years, so exactly when it started is impossible to say. Certainly it was in place in its matured form by the end of the 11th century.

The shires were divided into hundreds, which were in turn subdivided into tithings. Each tithing consisted of ten or twelve men, and was led by a tithingman. Needless to say, it was rarely as tidy as that. South of the Thames, the tithing was sometimes the entire township; in Hertfordshire, there were usually several tithings to the township. As with the kinship and the guild, the whole tithing was responsible for the behaviour of its members.

After the 12th century, frankpledge was more tightly enforced. Henry II's Assize of Clarendon in 1166 made the Sheriff became responsible for ensuring that all who were eligible were members of a tithing, and special sittings of the Hundred Court were held twice a year for the purpose. This examination was called the *view of frankpledge*. Every free man over the age of 12 years had to join a tithing, provided he had lived in his manor for at least a year. For example, in 1332 John le Man, aged twelve, was placed into the tithing of Adam le Man and sworn at Wymondley. Though being part of a tithing was compulsory for the majority, unsurprisingly there were exemptions for the wealthy and powerful.

The failing in all these law enforcement methods was that they relied at least to some extent on people informing on their friends, neighbours and even their own family, which of course many people were not prepared to do.

Hue and Cry

Hue and cry had its roots in the Anglo-Saxon period with the *clamour violentiae*. The principle was that if a crime was witnessed, there was a legal duty on the witness to raise hue and cry, and to pursue and arrest the offender. All able-bodied men over the age of 15 years who heard the hue and cry were obliged to join it. Should the pursuit cross a parish boundary, that parish must take up the pursuit as well. Where crimes were committed without a witness, the victim was left to deal with the offence as best he could.

The fugitive was in a difficult position. If he surrendered, he would be brought before a court, but he would have no right to speak in his own defence. The assumption was that, as the crime had been witnessed, he was guilty. If he resisted arrest however, he could be cut down.

A statute of 1252 described how hue and cry functioned:

> "Pursuit by hue and cry is to be made according to the ancient and proper form, so that those who neglect to follow the cry may be taken [to be] accomplices of the evildoers, and be delivered to the Sheriff. Moreover, in every town, four or six men, according to the number of the inhabitants, shall be appointed to make the hue and cry with promptitude and perseverance, and to pursue evildoers, if any should appear, with bows and arrows and other light weapons; which weapons ought to be provided for the custody of the whole town, and to remain for the use of the aforesaid town."

The Statute of Westminster in 1285 placed a duty on all men between 15 and 60 to keep arms in his house for the maintenance of the peace.

Hue and cry remained in active use for many years. In 1678 Nathaniell Ward, the constable of Ware, was indicted for not raising hue and cry after a suspected murderer. A few years later Henry Duck, one of the constables of Sawbridgeworth, was prosecuted for "not sending huan cry away that wase in pursuit of two shollgers (soldiers) that run from thear cullers (colours) from Hoddesdon."

Hue and cry was repealed in 1827, but sixty years later the Sheriffs' Act reintroduced a duty on the populace to assist in the arrest of felons; that requirement exists today, as an obligation to assist a police officer if requested to do so. Interestingly, though there is this requirement to assist, the civilian does not have the same immunities from prosecution the police officer has. A civilian can also make an arrest without the presence of a police officer in certain circumstances.

Parish Constables, Watch & Ward

Watch and ward was a legal duty for each community to establish a system to protect the town from criminals. A specified number of men guarded the town by day and by night. Henry III passed several laws on the matter, from 1233 onwards, and these were reissued, with amendments, under the Statute of Winchester in 1285.

Right: watchmen of the 16th century. Both men are armed, and carry lanterns. In addition the man on the left has a hand bell. From a 19th century print.

Large towns had to be walled, and watchmen set at every gate. The number to guard each gate was specified, and depended in part upon the size of the town. Anyone attempting to enter at night was arrested. They were released the following morning if found free from suspicion.

Watch and ward was a duty that applied to all able-bodied men, and was not always popular. In 1677 Richard Kidd of Hitchin not only refused to keep watch and ward, but he persuaded his neighbours to refuse as well.

In St. Albans during the 18th century, the watchmen had a shelter behind the clock tower. It must have been a boon in wet or winter weather.

Watchmen survived until the 19th century, though by then they were paid for their labours. The last watchman at Berkhamsted carried a truncheon and a rattle. His rounds lasted from 10.00 p.m. until dawn. His role was not merely to deter crime, but to assist in other ways too - raising the alarm in the event of fire, or escorting a drunk to his door for example.

Right: a rattle used to sound the alarm. It was eventually replaced by the whistle. (Hertfordshire Constabulary)

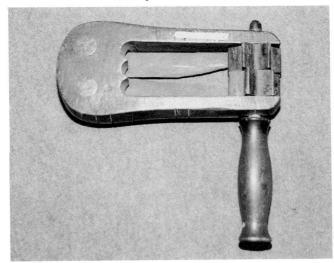

Henry Nash, writing in 1890 of events some fifty years before, says that this particular watchman was accosted one evening by a dog, and they quickly made friends. It accompanied him on his rounds that night until dawn. It reappeared promptly at 10.00 p.m. the following night, and again they did the rounds together. This pattern once established lasted for some years. The dog was eventually found to come from Potten End, about two miles out of town.

Parish constables as peace officers date at least from the Statute of Westminster in 1285, though the title is much older. Every hundred had a chief constable, beneath whom were appointed the petty constables.

The post was unpaid, hard work, and highly unpopular. According to Daniel Defoe, writing in the early 18th century, it was not unknown for constables to be made destitute, having neglected their own affairs in order to carry out their official duties. Apart from keeping the peace and tracking down criminals, the constable had to

- collect rates and taxes
- check that commodities were not being sold under weight
- organise watch and ward
- make sure that the cage and stocks were kept in good repair
- ensure that roads and bridges were in good repair
- collect presentments for the Assizes
- draw the ballot for who must serve in the militia
- carry out punishments and collect fines as directed by the Petty and Quarter Sessions.

Constables were selected annually by the Court Leet, or, later, by the Parish Vestry. In the early days there were property qualifications, so the candidates came from the landed classes; but later, nominees were allowed to pay a replacement to take their place. The result was predictable. "The stewards of several Leets, and the inhabitants of several parishes, do present inefficient men to be constables... such as cannot read nor write, prophane swearers and drunkards..."

An alternative to hiring a substitute was to buy a "Tyburn ticket." A person who had successfully prosecuted a felon was exempted from serving as a constable, and was given a certificate to that effect. These certificates were assignable, and a trade grew up in them. They were called Tyburn tickets after the gallows at Tyburn; a felony was originally an offence for which the penalty was death.

Charles Coomes of Broxbourne, a blacksmith, was granted such a dispensation in 1826, exempting him from "all manner of Parish and Ward Offices within... Broxbourne" as a result of having apprehended and prosecuted one William Holder, for the crime of burglary. Coomes sold his rights to James Poulter for "ten pounds of lawful money" two years later.

Yet not all constables were incompetent, or paid someone else to do the job. Thomas Crumion of Wheathampstead had already been constable three times when, at the age of seventy, he petitioned to be excused a fourth term, as he was "lame in one arm."

If the situation demanded it, special constables were sworn in. A letter to the constables of St. Andrews, Hertford, 21 October 1697:

"...whereas it is manifest that the roads are so infested with robbers, that it is highly dangerous for persons to travel with any quantity or sum of money... [you are] to provid five or six able men, without horses... well armed with muscots, carbines or guns... to be ready in the Market Place in Hertford to-moro morning... by halfe an ouer after six of the clock in the morning..."

Eventually, the constable came to be paid by a system of fees, and countrywide the system was abused, with fraudulent claims being made. Hertfordshire was no different, and in 1719 it was reported that as a result of abuses in charging for the lodging and conveying of vagrants, fixed fees would henceforth be paid: "for the lodging and relief of every single person for one night, 4d.; for a man and wife or two men and two women together, 6d., and 2d. apiece for their children... for every horse on which they shall convey such vagrants, 3d. a mile." Every day they spent conveying the vagrants towards their parish of settlement earned the constables the sum of 1s. 6d.

Other expenses that appear in the session rolls between 1795 and 1820 include

taking an oath on swearing in as constable	1s.
serving militia warrants	6d. each.
drawing and swearing militia	5s. a time.
attending four Quarter Sessions	6s.
apprehension of an offender	between 5s. and 10s.
administering a flogging	between 2s. 6d. and 10s.
searching the lodging houses of the borough of St. Albans	2s. 6d.

In addition, expenses incurred by the constable could be reclaimed; for example, the hire of horses and carts, and payments for the use of turnpike roads. Loss of earnings might also be allowed, though the justices were very aware of potentially fraudulent claims.

The 19th century saw the end of the parish constable and the birth of the county police force. Other methods of law enforcement had been running alongside the constables however, some working better than others.

Thief-Takers

Thief-takers were the bounty hunters of the 18th century. A private individual hired a thief-taker to track down a criminal, or recover stolen goods. That such an arrangement resulted in frequent abuses should have been a surprise to nobody. Unscrupulous thief-takers either paid someone to commit offences, or committed them themselves, then approached the victim with an offer of help. The most famous of these men was Jonathan Wilde, the self-styled "Thief-taker General," whose criminal organisation in London was widespread. A more callous individual is hard to imagine; he seems to have had no interest or concern for anyone but himself.

*Right: Jonathan
Wilde, the Thief-
Taker General.
Note the pillory,
gallows and stocks
beneath the
portrait. (Picture
source unknown)*

Wilde was responsible for sending at least 87 felons to the gallows, and the transportation to America of a further 30. He was born in Wolverhampton in 1682, and before becoming a thief-taker had been a bucklemaker and brothel keeper. A large part of his income was derived from "rewards" for the recovery of stolen goods – goods that he had arranged to be stolen by his criminal accomplices. Wilde's popularity declined when in 1724 he turned in Jack Sheppard, a highwayman hero worshipped by many of the poorer classes. Sheppard hanged at Tyburn.

The following year Wilde was arrested for rescuing one of his men from the constables. Further evidence came to light, and Henry Kelly and Margaret Murphy turned King's evidence in a case concerning stolen lace. He died on the gallows on 24 May 1725 in the company of two highwaymen and a coiner. His death was followed by an immediate decline in capital convictions.

Rewards

Rewards for the apprehension of criminals were offered by both the authorities, private individuals and associations. The government in the 18th century offered the substantial reward of £40 for the conviction of highwaymen, such was the magnitude of the problem.

From the end of the 18th century, private associations were formed, offering rewards for conviction of felons in their own area. There were associations in many Hertfordshire towns - Great Berkhamsted and Northchurch, Stevenage and Hatfield, Hertford, Baldock, and Tewin amongst them. Most disappeared soon after the formation of the county police force, though a few hung on for a while as social organisations.

The reliance on rewards as part of their income encourages constables and watchmen to concentrate on offences that would bring them the most cash. In some cases offenders were "set up" by the officers of the law, who encouraged them to commit crimes, or placed them in circumstances where their conviction was a foregone conclusion. In 1816 a major scandal broke in London, when three young Irishmen were arrested by officers apparently in the act of counterfeiting coins. In fact the evidence had been planted. Astonishingly the young men did not explain the circumstances in court, and it was only as a result of the vigilance of the magistrate that the truth came to light.

The Bow Street Runners

Some mention must be made of the Bow Street Runners, formed by Henry Fielding in London in the early 1750's. Fielding's interest in crime also resulted in a treatise which appeared in 1750 entitled "Inquiry into the Causes of the Late Increase of Robbers," which he attributed to drunkenness, and places of entertainment and music, "where the meanest person who can dress himself well might mix with his betters." After Henry Fielding's death in 1754 the Runners were taken over by his half-brother John. The first men were paid a guinea a week, plus rewards. In 1763 they formed a mounted patrol, and by 1805 there were 60 men patrolling to a 20 mile radius from the centre of London: well into Hertfordshire. Their red waistcoats earned them the nickname robin red breasts. Despite a number of scandals and allegations of corruption, the Bow Street Runners for the most part performed a valuable service to the capital and surrounding areas.

The Watching and Lighting Act

In 1833 an act was passed which permitted towns with a population above 5,000 to employ watchmen on a formal basis. Amongst the towns that chose this option was Hemel Hempstead, though with a complement of only three men, how they would have handled a major incident is not clear. It was however a step towards a modern police force, with professional peacekeepers replacing the amateur parish constables and watchmen.

The Borough Police

In 1835 the Municipal Corporations Act was passed, obliging all boroughs to form police forces under the control of a watch committee. In Hertfordshire, Hertford and St. Albans were the boroughs affected, and both complied with the act: Hertford on 21 January 1836 and St. Albans on 23 July the same year. The watchmen and parish constables were discharged.

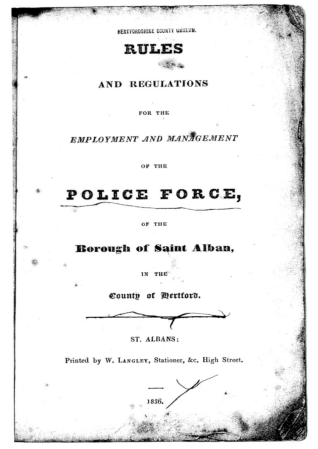

Right: Rules and Regulations for St. Albans Police from 1836. (the Museum of St. Albans)

HERTFORDSHIRE COUNTY MUSEUM.

RULES

AND REGULATIONS

FOR THE

EMPLOYMENT AND MANAGEMENT

OF THE

POLICE FORCE,

OF THE

Borough of Saint Alban,

IN THE

County of Hertford.

ST. ALBANS:

Printed by W. LANGLEY, Stationer, &c. High Street.

1836.

Hertford's force began with five men drafted from the Metropolitan Police. Within a few months, three had been sacked and the superintendent had resigned. The remaining officer was dismissed in 1840. It is possible that the Metropolitan Police had taken the opportunity to off-load some of their dead wood onto Hertford, who in their naivety accepted them.

Despite the problems the force quickly became popular as arrests were made. They remained independent until 1888, when, as Hertford had a population of less than 10,000, it was combined with the County Police.

St. Albans retained its independence much longer. Apart from a short period during the First World War, it held out until 1947. It was a success from the start, and there was a substantial reduction in the rate of crime in the town. The only problem was that the Petty Sessions for the Liberty of St. Albans insisted they had the right to make use of the Borough constables, though the Liberty paid nothing towards them.

Right: the badge of St. Albans City Police. (Museum of St. Albans)

The Night Constable's Book from the early years gives a flavour of the sort of cases the force dealt with:

20 September 1839	Daniel Epworth, labourer, from Plymouth, committed to the house of correction for 7 days with hard labour, for begging in Chequer Street.
17 January 1840	Oliver Hall, labourer, from Luton - drunk and treating his horse in a brutal manner in George Street. Also breaking to pieces the bedstead when under confinement in the cell. Fined 5s.

The picture was much the same some thirty years later; only 22 people were arrested for indictable offences, whilst 144 appeared before the magistrates for misdemeanours. The commonest offence was drunkenness (30) followed by assault (17).

In 1877 the St. Albans Borough Police became the St. Albans City Police. The badges on the helmets changed, but little else.

In 1890 officers from St. Albans were involved in a gun fight in Hatfield after being threatened by three armed men at the railway station. No-one was hurt, and one of the culprits was arrested at the scene. The others were detained later in London. Following this confrontation, sixty revolvers were bought for the county force. They were issued only to trusted officers, and were to be drawn only in self defence - a rare occurrence. The low level of armed crime is surprising, considering that there was no control of the sale of firearms until the 1920's. It may be that the relatively high cost of weapons made them unobtainable for the majority of petty criminals; or perhaps it was due to a difference in the criminal culture compared to later years.

At the time of the force's amalgamation with the County Force, the establishment was 65 men and 5 women.

The Parish Constables Act 1842

The Metropolitan Police were formed in 1829, and other police forces soon followed. The parish constable did not disappear immediately, however. As an alternative to police forces, the Parish Constables Act permitted counties to organise a system under which paid superintending constables supervised the old parish constables.

It was cheaper than forming a police force, although much less efficient. Buckinghamshire chose this route, and the result was that offenders from Hertfordshire used that county as a refuge. In return, Hertfordshire used Buckinghamshire as a dumping ground for vagrants and undesirables. The County and Borough Police Act of 1856 rendered the supervising constable arrangement obsolete.

The post of parish constable finally disappeared in 1872, though the option to re-appoint them in time of need was left open.

The County Force

The County Police Act of 1839 was an enabling act. The counties did not have to form a police force, but if they wished to do so that option was made available to them.

The debate sparked off across the county was a bitter one. The towns were generally for a police force; rural areas were against. Then, as now, country people believed that a police force would be unable to patrol what was then a largely rural county. The countryman would be subsidising the urban dweller.

None was more bitterly opposed than the Marquis of Salisbury. Unfortunately for his cause, he was not the best of speakers - at one debate "the Marquis of Salisbury in opposition to it broke completely down and cut a poor figure..."

The views of the justices were sought and considered, and the final vote at Quarter Sessions was close - 34 voted for a constabulary, 30 against.

At an estimated annual cost of over £5,000, Hertfordshire Constabulary was formed on 12 April 1841. With a strength of just 71 men, including the chief constable, they were going to be stretched.

Initially the force was unpopular. The rural areas resented them, and the justices that had voted against formation were unlikely to co-operate either. The Liberty of St. Albans was enthusiastic though. Their status as a liberty had left them out of the force, and they had had to petition parliament for inclusion.

The constable's uniform consisted of a blue serge belted coat, with white buttons, and a white embroidered collar. Trousers matched, and, to emphasise the non-military nature of the police, the ensemble was completed with a top hat. Helmets were suggested as early as 1864, but were not issued until almost 30 years later (straw helmets were issued for use in the summer.) A new uniform was provided once a year, and an allowance of 1s. 6d. per month was made for boots. The constable on patrol carried handcuffs and a rattle to call for help in time of need. Whistles were issued at a later date. At night he carried a lantern.

A variety of weapons were carried. The truncheon was introduced from the start, and cutlasses were sometimes issued. Firearms, though readily available until 1922 without a licence, were used only in exceptional circumstances.

Above: a .45 inch revolver believed to be part of a batch bought in the early 1890's. It is marked "Taylor and Son, Ironmongers and Co., Hertford," and "Herts Constabulary. Webley MP." (Hertfordshire Constabulary)

From the 1860's the Webley company specialised in police revolvers in various calibres, normally in the range .442 to .450. They were generally short-barrelled, and accurate over a short distance only. Later, the police adopted the .455 and .38 Webley & Scott and Enfield military revolvers, and later still Smith & Wesson revolvers in .38 special. Revolvers were replaced by 9mm self-loading pistols after the Second World War. Rifles were issued from time to time, but were normally used for shooting out-of-control animals rather than for law enforcement. Models adopted were military patterns, with the Lee Enfield series in .303 calibre serving for many years.

Below: Hertfordshire Constabulary whistle and chain, numbered 233. (Hertfordshire Constabulary)

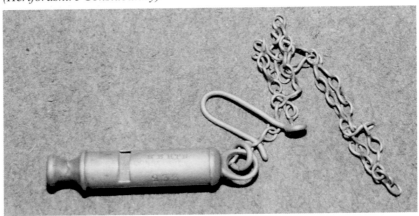

Above left: an officer's helmet. It replaced the stiffened top hat, right, in the 1890's. The helmet badge is numbered "3." (Hertfordshire Constabulary)

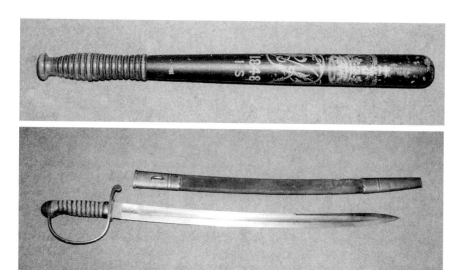

Top: a decorated ceremonial truncheon dated 1848. Bottom: a police cutlass and scabbard. (Hertfordshire Constabulary)

Handcuffs were supplied by a company called Hiatt, from 1800 the largest manufacturer in the country. They changed little in form for many years. Later models were nickel or chrome plated. Hiatt's handcuffs were simple and solid. There were no sharp edges to cut into the wrists. They were slow to apply however, and were superseded by models designed to overcome that problem. Unfortunately these cuffs did have sharp edges, and were painful for the prisoner.

Above, nineteenth century Hiatt handcuffs (Hertfordshire Constabulary)

Above: Another form of nineteenth century prisoner restraint: leg irons. (Hertfordshire Constabulary)

The statistics released after the first year of the force's formation won over some of the opposition. 50% of stolen property was recovered. 1,642 persons had been charged with offences, of whom 1,180 were convicted. In the whole of the Hatfield division, 55 square miles, only two sheep were stolen.

In 1853 the government formed a committee to consider policing throughout the country. They recommended that the formation of a county police force should be compulsory, and the County and Borough Police Act was passed in 1856. The main impact on Hertfordshire was that under the same act a quarter of pay and clothing was met by the government (increased to half in 1874).

The force was still responsible for some duties they had inherited from the parish constables. Weights and measures infringements, inspection of lodging houses, animal diseases; some of these duties persisted even into the middle of the 20th century. Some readers may recall posters concerning the colorado beetle, which, if found, had to be reported to the police.

In 1880 the force was reorganised from ten divisions into five: Bishop's Stortford, Hemel Hempstead, Hitchin, St. Albans (excluding the borough), and Ware. Training was centralised.

Telephone installation between stations began in 1891. The public could not call the police though: the system was between stations only. The system was inefficient, and it could take a considerable time to get a message from one station to another. The problems were not resolved until the end of the First World War.

Bicycles were introduced in the last decade of the 19th century, and a cycle corps set up, with a forage cap instead of a helmet. Motorcars followed, initially with a Wolsey for the chief constable. Later, procedures were put in place for hiring cars when necessary.

In 1900, the chief constable of Hertfordshire, Henry Daniells, ordered the destruction of all police records up to the year 1890. The reason was probably lack of storage space, but it was a tragedy nonetheless. Very little remains, but amongst that which does is the register of prisoners held in the cells at Baldock Police Station from 1886.

The number of prisoners is small (this one volume covers the years 1886 - 1922). The year 1888 was one of the more dramatic:

Peter Perry	Drunk and riotous at Baldock & wilfully breaking windows of police cell.
Henry Field	Stealing growing turnips at Norton.
Peter Perry (again)	Drunk and riotous at Baldock and assaulting the Police in the execution of their duty.
Bartholomew Clark	Deserting his child and leaving her chargeable to common fund of the Hitchin Union.
William Dixon	(Felony) by stealing a steel rule at Baldock the property of John Roberts value 1s. 9d.

And all this between 28 April and 24 November! Baldock was evidently a quiet place in those days. All the offenders were taken to Hitchin Police Station to be processed.

The first half of the 20th century was one of steady growth. The use of cars became more widespread, and the telephone system was sorted out. Following the First World War, resources became tight, and vacancies went unfilled. The establishment fell by 5%.

Of interest are the previous occupations of recruits. Between 1862 and 1912, 958 officers were appointed. Their backgrounds were as follows:

labourers	291
clerks	37
craftsmen	129
servants	236
other	265

Of these, 234 were dismissed for a variety of offences ranging from drunkenness to inefficiency.

For many years, military service was considered to be an asset to police officers (as it was to prison officers). Chief constables were appointed for their military background, which caused problems for them and the men they had to command.

The first plainclothes officer was appointed in 1892, at Watford, the main trouble spot in the county. In the past, officers had been seconded to criminal enquiries as required. Not until 1910 was a Criminal Investigation Department set up; until this point, like many other forces, Hertfordshire relied on the expertise of Scotland Yard to investigate serious offences.

In 1928 the first two women were appointed to the force, and in 1937 a fingerprint and photographic department was formed. The Constabulary was taking on the trappings of a modern force. Before their appointment, and in most cases for some time to come, officers' wives cared for female prisoners in police cells. They were expected to carry out other duties as well, and in some cases it was too much. Inspector Goodyear's wife was committed to the Three Counties Asylum in 1878, her insanity having been brought on by being shown the blood-soaked clothes of two murdered children.

The Second World War brought additional duties - air raid precautions, guarding of key installations, the checking of foreign nationals, and not least training Special Constables, Women's Auxiliary Police Reserve and the Police War Reserve (it was a War Reserve constable who arrested the spy, Karl Richter, in London Colney in 1941).

Hatfield Police Headquarters was damaged by a V1 bomb in 1944, and slight damage was suffered by a number of other stations.

As previously mentioned, shortly after the war the St. Albans City Police were absorbed by the County Force, and there we leave the Hertfordshire Police; mid-way into the 20th century, with at least the beginnings of a modern law enforcement agency; most of the departments we expect today either existed or were shortly to be founded, and the establishment had risen manyfold.

Police Stations

As with court buildings, there is insufficient space here to look at all the police stations in Hertfordshire. A small selection will have to suffice.

Some of the original stations - Berkhamsted and Hitchin - had been bridewells. In both cases new buildings have replaced them. The Victorian police station and magistrates' court in Hitchin still exists, however. It was completed in 1887, and is a fine example of its type.

The Tudor House in Old Welwyn used to be a police station. Built in 1540, it has also served as a Post Office and a chapel of rest. There is a long pole with a hook at one end that hangs beneath the first floor. It has been suggested that this was used for ducking witches. In fact, its purpose is to pull burning thatch from house roofs.

Hertford Borough Police's first station was in Mill Street, but such was the poor quality of workmanship that parts of it were declared unfit for habitation within thirty years of its erection. St. Albans' first station was behind the Town Hall.

Above: Watford's Police Station in St. Albans Road was built in 1896. The previous station had been in Talbot Road. This picture was taken in 1949. (Watford Observer)

Of the thirty-two purpose-built stations put up before 1962, sixteen were built before 1911. Most of the older ones are now gone, replaced by the soulless, but functional, structures put up in the last thirty years.

Investigation

In the early days of enforcement, investigative techniques scarcely existed. Prosecutions relied predominantly upon witness statements, and a great deal of reliance was placed upon the visual identification of suspects. Such investigators as existed were in effect spies. They cultivated criminals and their associates in the hope of bringing offenders to justice, and earning themselves a reward in the process.

The scientific study of crime and criminals began in the latter part of the 18th century. Lectures were given in Edinburgh on medical jurisprudence in 1792, and a professorship was established there in 1806.

New sciences, or in some cases pseudo-sciences, developed, falling under the umbrella of a new term - criminology. The criminologists studied all aspects of crime, including the offenders, the victims, methods of detection, criminal statistics, and punishment. Their objective was to apply the rationality of the new age to the investigation of crimes.

Early in the 19th century Franz Joseph Gall, then working in Paris, advanced the theory that criminal tendencies were innate. Criminals might be recognised, he suggested, by the shape of their skulls. The same idea was put forward by other Continental criminologists later in the century. Had this been true, it would have been possible to identify criminals before they knew it themselves. For many years the theory was highly popular; then in 1913 Dr. Charles Goring published his important work, *The English Criminal.* His studies of both criminal and non-criminal groups led him to the inevitable conclusion that there was no such thing as a criminal physical type (he used convicts and servicemen as his subjects).

In the same period fingerprints were studied, both in Britain and overseas. A number of systems were devised, all based on the original work of professor John Purkinje in Breslau in 1823; but it was the system of Sir Francis Galton that formed the basis of the modern method. He identified a number of features in fingerprints, and proposed a method of statistical analysis that seemed to guarantee the identification of individuals. Sixteen points of similarity between two prints indicated that they were made by the same person. In fact, reliance on the sixteen-point rule has occasionally led to misidentifications: it is important to look for differences between prints as well as correlations. Means of collecting latent prints, almost invisible to the naked eye, provided the investigator with an invaluable tool. He could now show that a suspect had touched specific objects: perhaps he had handled a weapon, or had visited a crime scene.

Identification of suspects assumed greater significance as it became clear that uncorroborated witness identification was unreliable. Scotland Yard issued a series of three photographs, apparently of the same man; their fingerprints proved that they were in fact of three different people. What chance then had a witness of identifying a suspect seen perhaps for only a few seconds? Successful prosecutions on such evidence alone became less common, but still occurred.

For a while, the science of anthropometry found favour as a means of identification. It was based on measurements of specific parts of the subject's body, and statistical analysis of them. Insofar as it went, the method was successful, but it had two main drawbacks. It could only be used to identify a suspect from whom a set of measurements had already been taken; and it was complex and time consuming, as it required numerous measurements to be made. Alphonse Bertillon of France developed a method of measurement and analysis that was used in a few countries well into the 20th century, though developments in fingerprinting techniques soon made it obsolete.

Above: though these photographs seem to be of the same person, they are of three different men. (Scotland Yard)

Handwriting too came under scrutiny under the science of graphology, though in the early days there were some spectacular failures. Bertillon, the advocate of anthropometry, also dabbled in the study of handwriting, and it was he who declared a letter in the famous Dreyfus case to be genuine. Alfred Dreyfus was accused of selling French military secrets to the Germans in the 1890's. Bertillon was wrong, and Dreyfus was sent to the French Guianan penal colony generally known as Devil's Island, in South America.

Each person's handwriting varies considerably depending upon his or her mood and situation. It changes too with time. It is difficult to say with certainty that two pieces of writing are by the same hand. Some graphologists went further: they claimed that the sex, appearance, age and social status of the writer could be established from his handwriting. It was even asserted by some that the subject's profession could be determined. By the mid 20th century, the less adventurous graphologists had established their respectability, and it was generally accepted that it was possible to make certain assertions. A forged signature could usually be identified, and samples of handwriting could be shown to bear a strong resemblance to another. Erasures and alterations showed up under the microscope. The study of the paper itself provided further opportunities to gather information. Even so, there was doubt expressed by some authorities about the value of such evidence.

Considerable advances were made in the first half of the 20th century in the study of firearms and their ammunition. Minute scratches and impressions are made by the breech, striker and rifling on both the cartridge case and bullet of each round fired. With microscopic examination it was established that not only every type of weapon, but the individual weapon itself was unique. It therefore became possible to identify the manufacturer, the model and the specific weapon in question, provided either bullet or cartridge case was found at the crime scene. Shotguns presented a problem however: their smooth bores left no rifling marks on the pellets, though cartridge cases could be tied to the gun that was used to fire them.

Law and Disorder in Hertfordshire

Advances in chemistry helped in a number of ways. Poisons could now be detected with some certainty. Bloodstains could be identified: initially as blood, then whether it was human or animal. The identification of blood types further aided investigation, but with a large proportion of the population having the same blood type, there were limits to its usefulness.

Chemical analysis and microscopic examination of samples taken from crime scenes advanced by leaps and bounds. All sorts of materials could be collected, investigated and identified, providing the investigator with scientific evidence that was difficult to refute in court.

Forensic medicine continued to play its part. Cause of death or injury could be established. The type of weapon, and sometimes the weapon itself could be matched to a wound. Time of death could be estimated with at least some degree of accuracy. Such variables as the temperature of the body, the degree of decay, even the stage within their life cycles that maggots and other insects had reached were studied to this end. Stomach contents were analysed. Improved medical and dental records allowed identification of victims even when soft tissues had decayed. By the end of our period, the middle of the 20th century, the forensic sciences had become some of the most important aids to criminal investigation.

Investigators in the 20th century increasingly specialised in particular types of offence - forgery, homicide, theft and so on. Techniques were exchanged between the police forces of different countries, and procedures crossed international boundaries. The methods of Hans Gross were widely followed, and his book, *System Der Kriminalistik*, appeared in many editions and many countries including Britain, under the title of *Criminal Investigation.*

Gross applied logic and common sense to the art of investigation. The detective should record everything and touch nothing until the recording was complete. Accuracy and precision in this recording were paramount. He should collect samples and witness statements; make comparisons and analyses of the information he gathered. Where necessary, he should draw on the knowledge of experts. Above all, he should keep an open mind until he had cause to change it.

Gross described in detail criminal techniques, their equipment and behaviour. He told the investigator of the pitfalls of his trade; how to interview witnesses; what was important, and what could be ignored. He explored types of evidence, from tooth marks to tyre treads, and how to collect and preserve samples for analysis. The range of Gross's book was comprehensive, and it became a manual for both the new and the established detective.

Thus by the mid-20th century, after little more than 150 years, investigation had developed from almost nothing to a sophisticated science, calling on the skills of specialists in a wide range of fields. The detective had many of the tools of the trade he needed. Further dramatic advances were in the future:

genetic fingerprinting and psychological analysis are only two examples. Given the time and manpower, many cases that in the past were unsolvable could now be unravelled.

Glossary

affreerer	one of two persons who assess fines as members of the jury in a Manor Court.
alderman	see ealdorman
amercement	a fine.
approver	an offender who turns King's evidence and implicates others in his crime in return for a reprieve. Enough 'accomplices' could in theory earn a pardon.
Assize, Court of	a senior court, ranking between the Quarter Sessions and the King's Bench; or an enactment with legal force, for example the *Assize* of Bread and Ale.
attainder, bill of	a bill depriving the accused of certain property rights.
baston	a weapon with a long shank, often with a point or points at one end.
bohr	Anglo-Saxon form of bail for appearance in court
bot	Anglo-Saxon: atonement to victim.
bridewell	see house of correction.
cage	a small lock-up, for minor offences such as drunkenness.
canon law	a system of law used by ecclesiastical courts until Henry VIII's split with Rome.
ceorl	Anglo-Saxon: a freeman, who is not a noble; a villein or sokeman.
clergy, benefit of	system exempting clerics and clergy from trial and punishment.
Commission of the Peace	appointment of justices to hold sessions for the keeping of the peace within a county or liberty.
Common Law	law based originally upon custom rather than statute.
Common Pleas, Court of	a central court, sitting permanently. In the 13th Century it was to separate from the King's Bench, only to be recombined in 1873.
compurgator	a witness swearing to the innocence of the accused
corruption of the blood, bill of	a bill incurring the loss of inheritance.
County Court	either the old Shire Court under another name, or a much more recent civil court.
court of record	a court whose decisions are binding upon other courts.
Crown Court	replacement for the Courts of Assize and Quarter Sessions in 1972.
Curia Regis	King's Court.
Danelaw	the part of Britain ruled by the Danes.
double jeopardy	a principle under which an accused could only be tried

	once for a single crime.
ealdorman, alderman	the chief legal officer of a Shire.
felony	a serious offence, originally meriting the death sentence.
folkesmote	Anglo-Saxon: a meeting of the people in formal session.
frankpledge	system of assigning responsibility for offences committed within a tithe.
Gaol Delivery	trial of prisoners held on criminal charges.
gemot	Anglo-Saxon: a meeting.
Grand Jury	a jury that decided whether there was a case to answer, and laid charges on behalf of the populace.
hide	a land measurement of about 120 acres.
house of correction	a local prison, originally for confinement of rogues and vagabonds.
hundred	a division of a county or shire, consisting of 100 tithes.
hundredman	the bailiff of a hundred.
ignoramus	a grand jury verdict meaning no case to answer.
in mercy	fined instead of a more severe penalty.
indictable offence	a more serious offence, triable at Crown Court.
indictment	a formal accusation of a crime.
King's Bench	initially heard cases of royal concern, or offenders with a right to be tried by him. In time it began to concentrate on criminal cases, though civil suits were still heard. It also corrected errors of lower courts.
King's Peace	either the peace of the land as a whole, or disturbance of the King, for which a heavy fine was levied.
liberty	a manor or a lordship with a charter making it independent of the hundreds.
misdemeanour	an offence less serious than a felony.
oubliette	an underground cell with no access other than from the top. From the French, *oublier*, to forget.
outlaw	one outside the law's protection.
Oyer and Terminer	a court of criminal jurisdiction for cases breaking the King's Peace.
page	a youth in the personal service of a person of rank.
Panopticon	a prison design by Jeremy Bentham.
Petty Sessions	a Justice of the Peace sitting alone.
presentment	a report by a constable or jury concerning a crime.
Quarter Sessions	a court between the Petty Sessions and Court of Assize.
recognizance	a bond for good behaviour.
reeve	representative for king or lord in court.
rolls	records of a court, e.g. Quarter Session Rolls.

separate system	of imprisonment, where prisoners are not permitted any form of association with each other. Compare with the Silent System.
sheriff	shire-reeve - the king's representative in the shire, or county court.
silent system	of imprisonment, where prisoners are not permitted to speak to each other, but work together under supervision. Compare with Separate System.
sokeman	*see ceorl.*
Star Chamber	criminal court originally dealing with violation of royal proclamations.
summary offence	a minor offence, normally dealt with by magistrates.
swainmote	one of the Forest Courts
tithe	a group of ten or twelve men, part of frankpledge.
transportation	the practice of sending convicted persons overseas.
true bill	there is a case to answer according to grand jury.
Unitarianism	the belief that God is a single entity, and rejects the Holy Trinity.
vacation	that part of the year when the law courts do not sit.
vestry	a method of local government, based on the local church administration, following the decline of manor courts.
villein	*see ceorl.*
virgate	one quarter of a hide, i.e. 30 acres.
wapentake	in Danelaw, the equivalent to a hundred.
wer, wer-gild	Anglo-Saxon: a man's value, based upon his rank in society. The fine payable in the event of a man's death.
witan	Anglo-Saxon: the royal council.
wite, wita	Anglo-Saxon: fine payable to the crown.
witenage	Anglo-Saxon: the king's court, or council of advisors.
witenagemot	Anglo-Saxon: the meeting of the king's council.
woodmote	one of the Forest Courts
yeoman	a free man who cultivated his own land.

Money and Measures

For those unfamiliar with the Imperial system of weights and measures, and "pounds, shillings and pence," here are explanations and conversions for some of those most commonly encountered.

Money

1 pound = 20 shillings
1 shilling = 12 pence
1 penny = 4 farthings
1 crown = 5 shillings
1 guinea = 21 shillings
1 mark = 13 shillings and 4 pence

Land Measures and Lengths

1 hide = 4 virgates
1 virgate = 30 acres
1 acre = 4840 square yards
1 mile = 1760 yards
1 furlong = 220 yards
1 chain = 22 yards
1 yard = 3 feet
1 foot = 12 inches

Volume

1 gallon = 8 pints
1 quart = 2 pints

Weight

1 ton = 20 stone (abbreviated to cwt.)
1 stone = 14 pounds (abbreviated to lb.)
1 pound = 16 ounces (abbreviated to oz.)

Conversions

1 metre = 39 inches
1 mile = 1.61 kilometres
1 acre = 4047 square metres
1 pound = 0.454 kilograms
1 gallon = 4.55 litres

Bibliography

Adams, George Burton *Constitutional History of England* Jonathan Cape 1935

Alderman, H. M. *A Pilgrimage in Hertfordshire* The Book Castle 1997

Ashworth, Andrew *Principles of Criminal Law* O. U. Press 1995

Bayes, W. O. *Crime and Punishments - A Thesis* Barnet 1901

Beachcroft, T. O. & Emms, W. B. *Five Hide Village* Datchworth Parish
    Council 1984

Billett, Michael *Highwaymen and Outlaws* Arms & Armour Press 1997

Bland, James *The Common Hangman* Ian Henry Publications 1984

Branch Johnson, W. *Hertfordshire* B. T. Batsford 1970

Branch Johnson, W., Ed. *Memorandums For...The Carrington Diaries*
    Phillimore & Co. Ltd. 1973

Chauncy, Henry *The Historical Antiquities of Hertfordshire* 1700

Chesney, Kellow *The Victorian Underworld* Temple Smith 1970

Clarkson, C. M. V. *Understanding Criminal Law* Fontana Press 1987

Cobb, Rev. J. *History and Antiquities of Berkhamsted* The Bookstack 1988

Cockburn, J.S. *Calendar of Hertfordshire Assize Records, Vols I & II, Eliz. I &
    James I* HMSO 1975

Crellin, Vivian *A Market Town in Tudor Times* Egon 1995

Crellin, Vivian *Baldock's Middle Ages* Egon 1995

Curtis, Gerald *A Chronicle of Small Beer* Phillimore 1970

de Smith, S. A. *Constitutional and Administrative Law* Penguin Books 1977

Dean, David *St. Albans Quarter Sessions Rolls 1784-1820* Hertfordshire
    Record Publications 1991

Denning, Lord *Landmarks in the Law* Butterworth & Co. 1984

Farris, Noel *The Wymondleys* Hertfordshire Publications 1989

Foster, Anthony M. *The Book of Hitchin* Barracuda Books, 1981

Foster, Anthony M. *Market Town* E & E Plumridge Ltd. 1987

Garland, David *Punishment and Welfare - A History of Penal Strategies*
    Gower Publishing Co Ltd 1985

Gerish, W. B. *Hertfordshire Folklore* S. R. Publishers Ltd., 1970

Griffin, Ken *Transported Beyond the Seas* Hertfordshire Family & Population
    Society 1997

Gross, Dr. Hans *Criminal Investigation* Sweet & Maxwell Ltd. 1949

Gutchen, Robert M., Truwert, Eleanor & Peters, Grace: *Down & Out in
    Hertfordshire - a Symposium on the Old and New Poor Law*
    Hertfordshire Publications 1984

Hackwood, Frederick W. *Inns, Ales and Drinking Customs of Old England*
    Bracken Books 1985

Haining, Peter *The English Highwayman* Robert Hale 1991

Harrison, Paul *Hertfordshire and Bedfordshire Murders* Countryside Books 1993

Hawkings, David T. *Criminal Ancestors* Alan Sutton Publishing Ltd. 1992

Hazlitt, W. C. *Dictionary of Faiths and Folklore* Reeves and Turner 1905

Hebditch, Felicity *A History of Victoria Square* St. Albans Irish Life Assurance, 1993

Hertfordshire Advertiser

Hertfordshire Countryside

Hertfordshire Express

Hertfordshire Federation of Women's Institutes *The Hertfordshire Village Book* Countryside Books 1986

Hertfordshire Mercury

Hewitt, John *Ancient Armour and Weapons in Europe* John Henry & James Parker, 1855

Hine, Reginald *The History of Hitchin, Vols I & II* Eric T Moore 1972

Hitchin Pictorial

Hole, Christina *Witchcraft in England* Charles Scibner's Sons 1947

Howard, John *The State of the Prisons* J M Dent & Sons Ltd 1929

Hughes, Geoffrey *Swearing* Blackwell 1991

Jones, Arthur, Ed. *Hertfordshire 1731-1800 as Recorded in the Gentleman's Magazine* Hertfordshire Publications 1993

Jones-Baker, Doris *Tales of Old Hertfordshire* Countryside Books 1987

Kingston, Alfred *A History of Royston* Elliot Stock 1906

Le Hardy, W. *Hertfordshire County Session Rolls, 1581-1698* Hertfordshire County Council 1905

Loyn, H. R. *The Church and the Law in Early Anglo-Saxon England* Vaughan Paper no. 37, University of Leicester, 1992

Low, Donald A. *The Regency Underworld* Sutton Publishing 1999

Mayhew, Henry *London's Underworld* Bracken Books 1983

Morgan, Kennet O. *The Oxford Illustrated History of Britain*, Oxford University Press, 1984

Munby, Lionel M. *The Poor People are Not Nothing* Hertfordshire Publications 1995

Nash, Henry *Reminiscences of Berkhamsted* The Bookstack 1988

Osborn, Neil *The Story of Hertfordshire Police* Hertfordshire Countryside 1970

Page, William (ed) *The Victoria History of the County of Hertford*, Constable & Co., 1902-12

Palmer, Anthony (ed) *Tudor Churchwardens Accounts* Hertfordshire Record Society 1985

Pigram, R. J. *A Felons Lot* Hertfordshire Countryside Vol. 22 No 101, 1967

Priestly, Philip *Victorian Prison Lives* Pimlico 1999

Pringle, Jim, and Treversh, Jim *150 Years Policing in Watford District and Hertfordshire County* Radley-Shaw 1991

Richards, Jeffrey *Sex, Dissidence and Damnation* Routledge 1991

Rollason, D. W. *Two Anglo-Saxon Rituals: Church Dedication and the Judicial Ordeal* Vaughan Paper no. 33, University of Leicester, 1987

Rook, Tony *A History of Hertfordshire* Phillimore & Co Ltd 1984

Rose, June *Elizabeth Fry* MacMillan 1980

Scott, George Rydley *A History of Corporal Punishment* Senate 1996

Scott, George Rydley *A History of Torture* T Werner Laurie 1940

Sporne, K. R. *An Illustrated Catalogue of Stocks in Great Britain,* privately published, 1988

Strube, K. Audrey *The Buntingford Cage* Hertfordshire Countryside Vol. 23 No 121, 1969

Stubbs, William *Select Charters Illustrative of English Constitutional History* Oxford University Press 1884

Symposium *The Peasants' Revolt in Hertfordshire 1381* Hertfordshire Publications 1981

Thompson, David *England in the Nineteenth Century* Penguin Books 1950

W. Percival Westell *Historic Hertfordshire* Stephen Austin Ltd. 1931

Webb, Sidney & Beatrice *English Prisons Under Local Government* Longmans Green & Co. 1922

Index

An entry in **bold** denotes an illustration.

Brown, Ellen, 10
Broxbourne, 12, 114
Burchmore, Anthony, 78
Burges, Mary, 10
Burgess, James, 103
Burgess, Joseph, 22
Burkbey, Christopher, 40
Burke & Hare, 31-31
burning to death, 4, 9, 11, 101, 106-7
Bushey, 10
Byrche, James, 109
Caddington, 75
cages and lockups: 53, 56, **66**, 66-70, **68-70**, 95, 114, 132
Calcott, E. J., 21
Caldercraft, William, 103
Camp, Nathaniel, 103
Canon law, 3, 132
capital punishment, 3, 4, 9, 11, **12**, 18, 20, 21, 22, 24, 25, 28, 32, 47, **102**, **105**, **106**, 101-107, 116 see also *beheading, boiling to death, burning, draw hang & quartering, hanging*
caps, compulsory wearing of, 30
Carnarvon Committee, 62, 63
Carrington, John, 20, 42, 94
Carter, John, 92
cat o' nine tails, **12**, 100
Catheral, John, 20
Cathrow family, **31**
Caxton Gibbet, 104, **104**,
Caxton, William, 9
Celtic law, 3
chains, hanging in, 103-104, **104**
Chapel-en-le-Frith, 94
Charing Cross, 22
Charles I, 13, 26
Charles II, 14, 15, 41
Chatham, 89
Chauncy, Henry, 37, 106
Chaunsie, Phillipa, 13
Cherry, Walter, 12
Cheshunt, 13, 23, 68
Chester, 96
Chester, Robert, 44
Children, 10, 14, 23, 24, 65, 94, 99, 115, 126
Children's Act (1907), 24, 65
chimney sweeps, 18, 23
Chipping Barnet, 41, 90
cholera, 56
circuit, court, 42, 45, 47
City Police, 119-120, **119**, 126
Civil War, English, 13,44

Clarendon Code, 14-15, 15
Clarendon, Assize of (1166), 38, 54, 110
Clarendon, Constitutions of (1164), 39
Clark, Bartholomew, 125
Clerks of Assize, 42, 45
Clerks of the Peace, 42, 45, 46
Clerks to the Justices, 45
Clopton, 27
Clopton, Lawrence of, 27
Cnute, 3, 6
Cockenhatch, 44
Coles Hill, 27
collar, **108**
Colley, Thomas, 18, 20
Colney, 109
Commission of the Peace, 46, 132
Common Law, 8, 9, 38, 43, 107, 132
Common Pleas, Court of, 38, 47, 132
Commonwealth, the, 2, 13
compter, 49, **49**, 85-86
compurgators, 33, 34, 38, 132
Contagious Diseases Prevention Act (1864), 28
Conventicle Act (1664), 15
Coomes, Charles, 114
Corbett, Richard, 40
corporal punishment, 3, 5, **12**, 18, 22, 37, 47, 64, 65, 85-86, **93**, 97-100, **99** see also *birch, cat o' nine tails, whipping*
County and Borough Police Act (1856), 120, 124
county bread, 55
County Court, 43, 49, 132, 134
County Court Act (1867), 43
County Police Act (1839), 120
Court Baron, 38, 47
Court Leet, 38, 47, 67, 96, 114
Cowle, Alice, 94
Cowper, Earl, 18
crank, 63, **64**, 65
Criminal Justice (Amendment) Act (1926), 47
Criminal Justice Acts, 65, 74
Criminal Law Amendment Act (1885), 29
criminology, 127-128
Criminal Investigation Department (CID),126
Criswell, W., 103
Cromwell, Oliver, 14
Croydon, 27
Crumion, Thomas, 114
Cubitt, William, 63
cucking stool, 96
Cummins, James, 22
Curia Regis, see *King's Court*
Cutler, Mr. (surgeon), 79

Books Published by THE BOOK CASTLE

CHANGES IN OUR LANDSCAPE: Aspects of Bedfordshire, Buckinghamshire and the Chilterns 1947-1992: Eric Meadows. Over 350 photographs from the author's collection spanning nearly 50 years.

COUNTRYSIDE CYCLING IN BEDFORDSHIRE, BUCKINGHAMSHIRE AND HERTFORDSHIRE: Mick Payne. Twenty rides on and off-road for all the family.

PUB WALKS FROM COUNTRY STATIONS: Bedfordshire and Hertfordshire: Clive Higgs. Fourteen circular country rambles, each starting and finishing at a railway station and incorporating a pub stop at a mid way point.

PUB WALKS FROM COUNTRY STATIONS: Buckinghamshire and Oxfordshire: Clive Higgs. Circular rambles incorporating pub-stops.

LOCAL WALKS: South Bedfordshire and North Chilterns: Vaughan Basham. Twenty-seven thematic circular walks.

LOCAL WALKS: North and Mid Bedfordshire: Vaughan Basham. Twenty-five thematic circular walks.

FAMILY WALKS: Chilterns South: Nick Moon. Thirty 3 to 5 mile circular walks.

FAMILY WALKS: Chilterns North: Nick Moon. Thirty shorter circular walks.

CHILTERN WALKS: Hertfordshire, Bedfordshire and North Bucks: Nick Moon.

CHILTERN WALKS: Buckinghamshire: Nick Moon.

CHILTERN WALKS: Oxfordshire and West Buckinghamshire: Nick Moon. A trilogy of circular walks, in association with the Chiltern Society. Each volume contains 30 circular walks.

OXFORDSHIRE WALKS: Oxford, the Cotswolds and the Cherwell Valley: Nick Moon.

OXFORDSHIRE WALKS: Oxford, the Downs and the Thames Valley: Nick Moon. Two volumes that complement Chiltern Walks: Oxfordshire, and complete coverage of the county, in association with the Oxford Fieldpaths Society. Thirty circular walks in each.

THE D'ARCY DALTON WAY: Nick Moon. Long-distance footpath across the Oxfordshire Cotswolds and Thames Valley, with various circular walk suggestions.

THE CHILTERN WAY: Nick Moon. A guide to the new 133 mile circular Long-Distance Path through Bedfordshire, Buckinghamshire, Hertfordshire and Oxfordshire, as planned by the Chiltern Society.

JOURNEYS INTO BEDFORDSHIRE: Anthony Mackay. Foreword by The Marquess of Tavistock, Woburn Abbey. A lavish book of over 150 evocative ink drawings.

COCKNEY KID & COUNTRYMEN: Ted Enever. The Second World War remembered by the children of Woburn Sands and Aspley Guise. A six year old boy is evacuated from London's East End to start life in a Buckinghamshire village.

BUCKINGHAM AT WAR: Pip Brimson. Stories of courage, humour and pathos as Buckingham people adapt to war.

WINGS OVER WING: The Story of a World War II Bomber Training Unit: Mike Warth. The activities of RAF Wing in Buckinghamshire.

JOURNEYS INTO BUCKINGHAMSHIRE: Anthony Mackay. Superb line drawings plus background text: large format landscape gift book.

BUCKINGHAMSHIRE MURDERS: Len Woodley. Nearly two centuries of nasty crimes.

WINGRAVE: A Rothschild Village in the Vale: Margaret and Ken Morley. Thoroughly researched and copiously illustrated survey of the last 200 years in this lovely village between Aylesbury and Leighton Buzzard.

HISTORIC FIGURES IN THE BUCKINGHAMSHIRE LANDSCAPE: John Houghton. Major personalities and events that have shaped the county's past, including Bletchley Park.

TWICE UPON A TIME: John Houghton. North Bucks short stories loosely based on fact.

SANCTITY AND SCANDAL IN BEDS AND BUCKS: John Houghton. A miscellany of unholy people and events.

MANORS and MAYHEM, PAUPERS and PARSONS: Tales from Four Shires: Beds., Bucks., Herts. and Northants: John Houghton. Little known historical snippets and stories.

THE LAST PATROL: Policemen killed on duty while serving the Thames Valley: Len Woodley.

FOLK: Characters and Events in the History of Bedfordshire and Northamptonshire: Vivienne Evans. Anthology of people of yesteryear - arranged alphabetically by village or town.

JOHN BUNYAN: His Life and Times: Vivienne Evans. Highly praised and readable account.

THE RAILWAY AGE IN BEDFORDSHIRE: Fred Cockman. Classic, illustrated account of early railway history.

A LASTING IMPRESSION: Michael Dundrow. A boyhood evacuee recalls his years in the Chiltern village of Totternhoe near Dunstable.

GLEANINGS REVISITED: Nostalgic Thoughts of a Bedfordshire Farmer's Boy: E.W. O'Dell. His own sketches and early photographs adorn this lively account of rural Bedfordshire in days gone by.

BEDFORDSHIRE'S YESTERYEARS Vol 2: The Rural Scene: Brenda Fraser-Newstead. Vivid first-hand accounts of country life two or three generations ago.

BEDFORDSHIRE'S YESTERYEARS Vol 3: Craftsmen and Tradespeople: Brenda Fraser-Newstead. Fascinating recollections over several generations practising many vanishing crafts and trades.

BEDFORDSHIRE'S YESTERYEARS Vol 4: War Times and Civil Matters: Brenda Fraser-Newstead. Two World Wars, plus transport, law and order, etc.

DUNNO'S ORIGINALS: A facsimile of the rare pre-Victorian history of Dunstable and surrounding villages. New preface and glossary by John Buckledee, Editor of The Dunstable Gazette.

PROUD HERITAGE: A Brief History of Dunstable, 1000-2000AD: Vivienne Evans. Century by century account of the town's rich tradition and key events, many of national significance.

DUNSTABLE WITH THE PRIORY: 1100-1550: Vivienne Evans. Dramatic growth of Henry I's important new town around a major crossroads.

DUNSTABLE IN TRANSITION: 1550-1700: Vivienne Evans. Wealth of original material as the town evolves without the Priory.

DUNSTABLE DECADE: THE EIGHTIES: A Collection of Photographs: Pat Lovering. A souvenir book of nearly 300 pictures of people and events in the 1980's

STREETS AHEAD: An Illustrated Guide to the Origins of Dunstable's Street Names: Richard Walden. Fascinating text and captions to hundreds of photographs, past and present, throughout the town.

DUNSTABLE IN DETAIL: Nigel Benson. A hundred of the town's buildings and features, plus town trail map.

OLD DUNSTABLE: Bill Twaddle. A new edition of this collection of early photographs.

BOURNE and BRED: A Dunstable Boyhood Between the Wars: Colin Bourne. An elegantly written, well illustrated book capturing the spirit of the town over fifty years ago.

OLD HOUGHTON: Pat Lovering. Pictorial record capturing the changing appearances of Houghton Regis over the past 100 years.

ROYAL HOUGHTON: Pat Lovering. Illustrated history of Houghton Regis from the earliest of times to the present.

GIRLS IN BLUE: Christine Turner. The activities of the famous Luton Girls Choir properly documented over its 41 year period from 1936 to 1977.

THE STOPSLEY BOOK: James Dyer. Definitive, detailed account of this historic area of Luton. 150 rare photographs.

THE STOPSLEY PICTURE BOOK: James Dyer. New material and photographs make an ideal companion to The Stopsley Book.

PUBS and PINTS: The Story of Luton's Public Houses and Breweries: Stuart Smith. The background to beer in the town, plus hundreds of photographs, old and new.

LUTON AT WAR - VOLUME ONE: As compiled by the Luton News in 1947, a well illustrated thematic account.

LUTON AT WAR - VOLUME TWO: Second part of the book compiled by The Luton News.

THE CHANGING FACE OF LUTON: An Illustrated History: Stephen Bunker, Robin Holgate and Marian Nichols. Luton's development from earliest times to the present busy industrial town. Illustrated in colour and mono.

WHERE THEY BURNT THE TOWN HALL DOWN: Luton, The First World War and the Peace Day Riots, July 1919: Dave Craddock. Detailed analysis of a notorious incident.

THE MEN WHO WORE STRAW HELMETS: Policing Luton, 1840-1974: Tom Madigan. Fine chronicled history, many rare photographs; author served in Luton Police for fifty years.

BETWEEN THE HILLS: The Story of Lilley, a Chiltern Village: Roy Pinnock. A priceless piece of our heritage - the rural beauty remains but the customs and way of life described here have largely disappeared.

KENILWORTH SUNSET: A Luton Town Supporter's Journal: Tim Kingston. Frank and funny account of football's ups and downs.

A HATTER GOES MAD!: Kristina Howells. Luton Town footballers, officials and supporters talk to a female fan.

LEGACIES: Tales and Legends of Luton and the North Chilterns: Vic Lea. Mysteries and stories based on fact, including Luton Town Football Club. Many photographs.

THREADS OF TIME: Shela Porter. The life of a remarkable mother and businesswoman, spanning the entire century and based in Hitchin and (mainly) Bedford.

STICKS AND STONES: The Life and Times of a Journeyman Printer in Hertford, Dunstable, Cheltenham and Wolverton: Harry Edwards.

LEAFING THROUGH LITERATURE: Writers' Lives in Herts and Beds: David Carroll. Illustrated short biographies of many famous authors and their connections with these counties.

A PILGRIMAGE IN HERTFORDSHIRE: H.M. Alderman. Classic, between-the-wars tour round the county, embellished with line drawings.

THE VALE OF THE NIGHTINGALE: Molly Andrews. Several generations of a family, lived against a Harpenden backdrop.

SUGAR MICE AND STICKLEBACKS: Childhood Memories of a Hertfordshire Lad: Harry Edwards.Vivid evocation of gentle pre-war in an archetypal village, Hertingfordbury.

SWANS IN MY KITCHEN: Lis Dorer. Story of a Swan Sanctuary near Hemel Hempstead.

THE HILL OF THE MARTYR: An Architectural History of St.Albans Abbey: Eileen Roberts. Scholarly and readable chronological narrative history of Hertfordshire and Bedfordshire's famous cathedral. Fully illustrated with photographs and plans.

CHILTERN ARCHAEOLOGY: RECENT WORKS: A Handbook for the Next Decade: Edited by Robin Holgate. The latest views, results and excavations by twenty-three leading archaeologists throughout the Chilterns.

THE TALL HITCHIN INSPECTOR'S CASEBOOK: A Victorian Crime Novel Based on Fact: Edgar Newman. Worthies of the time encounter more archetypal villains.

SPECIALLY FOR CHILDREN

VILLA BELOW THE KNOLLS: A Story of Roman Britain: Michael Dundrow. An exciting adventure for young John in Totternhoe and Dunstable two thousand years ago.

THE RAVENS: One Boy Against the Might of Rome: James Dyer. On the Barton Hills and in the south-east of England as the men of the great fort of Ravensburgh (near Hexton) confront the invaders.

THE BOOK CASTLE, 12 Church Street, Dunstable,
Bedfordshire LU5 4RU
Tel: (01582) 605670 Fax (01582) 662431
Email: bc@book-castle.co.uk

JOURNEYS INTO HERTFORDSHIRE
by Anthony Mackay

This collection of nearly 200 ink drawings depicts the buildings and landscape of the still predominantly rural county of Hertfordshire. After four years of searching, the author presents his personal choice of memorable images, capturing the delights of a hitherto relatively unfeted part of England.

The area is rich in subtle contrasts - from the steep, wooded slopes of the Chilterns to the wide-open spaces of the north-east and the urban fringes of London in the south. Ancient market towns, an impressive cathedral city and countless small villages are surrounded by an intimate landscape of rolling farmland.

The drawings range widely over all manner of dwellings from stately home to simple cottage and over ecclesiastical buildings from cathedral to parish church. They portray bridges, mills and farmsteads, chalk downs and watery river valleys, busy street scenes and secluded village byways.

The accompanying notes are deliberately concise but serve to entice readers to make their own journeys around this charming county.

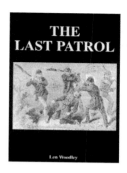

THE LAST PATROL
Policemen Killed on Duty while Serving
in the Thames Valley
by Len Woodley

This book details those Policemen who have been killed on duty by a criminal act within the area now covered by the Thames Valley Police - namely the counties of Berkshire, Buckinghamshire and Oxfordshire. It ranges from a Constable who, in the 1860s, died in Oxford just days after the formation of one of the constituent forces that made up the present-day Thames Valley Police and must surely be one of the shortest serving Policemen in this country, to the truly terrible day at Hungerford in the late 1980s, when so many people, including a traffic Constable, were murdered and others wounded in that picturesque Berkshire town. It encompasses Police officers encountering poachers, ejecting some drunken men from a public house, checking details of members of the visiting forces involved in a fracas in wartime England, attempting the apprehension of burglars and questioning some vicious, "stop at nothing" criminals over their behaviour in a motor car.

These police officers all started their day as normal, not one gave a thought to the possibility that he might be sent to a life-threatening job.

BUCKINGHAMSHIRE MURDERS
by Len Woodley

Thoroughly researched accounts of seventeen murders ranging across the old County of Buckinghamshire. Commencing from the early nineteenth century right up to modern times. You will read about the Newton Longville shop-keeper murdered for a few shillings; the Dagnall killer; murders for no apparent reason at Buckingham and Denham; the unsolved murder of the canal man at Slough; love affairs that went tragically wrong at Burnham and Bourne End; a fatal ambush at Botolph Claydon; the Pole who wanted to be shot and a fellow country-man who escaped justice by fleeing to the Soviet Union. There is the trooper who slew his girlfriend at Slough and hid the body under the mattress; the W.R.A.F girl who offered to baby-sit but met a killer instead; the bright young girl who went for a last walk down a country lane and the couple who were the victims of a man's obsession with himself!

POLICING LUTON 1840-1974

THE MEN WHO WORE STRAW HELMETS
by T.J. Madigan

This is the meticulously chronicled story of Luton's citizens and their Policemen - from the town's humble Parish beginnings in the early nineteenth century to its County Borough status over one hundred and thirty-five years later. Luton's fiercely independent streak is nowhere better evidenced than by its struggle to keep its Police Force separate from the rest of the County.

Chronological chapters gradually unfold the path of its growth in size and stature, taking in such landmark events as the Peace Riots of 1919 and the famous Luton Sack Murder of 1943. Throughout, valuable insights are given into the changing nature of general police procedures and legislation.

Dozens of rare photographs offer further fascinating glimpses into the past, and include several group pictures taken between 1895 and 1945. An appendix lists everyone who served from the time of the formation of the Force to its demise in 1947.

Tom Madigan reveals the special knowledge of a dedicated insider. He followed his father into the police and himself served from 1939 to 1987 in all five Forces in Luton under nine Chief Constables.

The Book Castle

STICKS & STONES
The Life and Times of a Journeyman Printer
Hertford, Dunstable, Cheltenham & Wolverton
by Harry Edwards

Sticks and Stones recounts the story of the author's journey through his life in the printing industry, from printer's devil until retirement. Leaving school at the age of fourteen, Harry's transition from schoolboy to apprentice was abrupt. The printing world, with its own language, customs and tradition, was strange at first but most of the journeymen were kind and helpful to a young lad, covering up for many a mistake in the first formative years.

The journey begins in Hertfordshire, then takes him on to Bedfordshire, Gloucestershire, London and finally to Buckinghamshire. It follows the author's progress as he seeks not only promotion but also the opportunity to become involved in the latest technology, be it cold type composition, photocomposition, or computer aided typesetting. He touches briefly on his private life when it is appropriate, but the story is primarily about how the changes in the printing industry affected him. The author is now retired and lives in Milton Keynes.

The Book Castle